RICK WARREN'S
BIBLE STUDY
METHODS

Also by Rick Warren

The Purpose Driven® Life

The Purpose Driven® Church

Living with Purpose Series

God's Answers to Life's Difficult Questions

God's Power to Change Your Life

RICK WARREN'S
BIBLE STUDY
METHODS

Twelve Ways You Can
Unlock God's Word

SPECIAL EDITION

From the author of
THE PURPOSE DRIVEN® LIFE

ZONDERVAN®

ZONDERVAN.com/
AUTHORTRACKER
follow your favorite authors

ZONDERVAN

Rick Warren's Bible Study Methods
Copyright © 1981, 2006, 2011 by Rick Warren

Formerly published under the title *Personal Bible Study Methods*

Requests for information should be addressed to:

Zondervan, *Grand Rapids, Michigan 49530*

This edition: ISBN 978-0-310-49593-2

Library of Congress Cataloging-in-Publication Data

Warren, Richard.
    Rick Warren's Bible study methods : Twelve ways you can unlock God's Word /
    Rick Warren.
       p. cm.
    ISBN 978-0-310-27300-4
    1. Bible — Study and teaching. I. Title.
    BS600.3.W37 2006
    220.071 – dc22   2005037198

Interior design: Mark Sheeres

Printed in the United States of America

11 12 13 14 15 16 17 18 /DCI/ 18 17 16 15 14 13 12 11 10 9 8 7 6 5 4 3 2 1

To my wife, *Elizabeth Kay,*

whose prayers, support, and commitment to

disciple-making have been a constant

encouragement while I was working on this book.

She is truly a gift from God.

CONTENTS

PREFACE

For many years every time I heard a good sermon or some in-depth Bible teaching, I would leave the meeting frustrated, wondering to myself, *How did he find all of that in his text?* I wanted to be able to discover those truths on my own. In addition, I often felt guilty because people were always telling me I ought to study the Bible, but when I tried to study it, I didn't know what to do. So I would get discouraged and give up.

Since those days of frustration, I have discovered that most Christians sincerely want to study their Bibles on their own, but they just don't know how. They don't need more exhortation ("You ought to study your Bible!"); they just need some instruction on how to study the Word of God. And that is the purpose of this book — it is a "how-to" manual on Bible study. It assumes that you already know the importance of personal Bible study, that you have been exhorted many times to this Christian duty, and that you have been waiting for someone to show you how to do it.

The Bible teaches us that we cannot be disciples of Jesus Christ if we do not have a regular intake of the Word of God. On one occasion Jesus said to his followers, "If you continue in my word, then are you my disciples indeed; and you shall know the truth, and the truth shall make you free" (John 8:31–32 KJV). As we look back through the history of the Christian church, we find that the common denominator of every great man and woman of God is that they knew the Scriptures and spent consistent, regular time with the Lord in his Word.

Never before in history has the Bible been more available to the Western world. Yet never before has there been such a famine of God's Word. We have Bibles in hotels, motels, doctors' offices, libraries, and most homes in America, yet most people are ignorant of what the Scriptures have to say. We live in a day of biblical illiteracy, even among many people of God.

Each study method in this book is presented in such a way that any believers in Christ can follow the steps suggested and be able *on their own* to get something out of their study of the Scriptures. I trust that your reading, study, and use of this book will make you into a biblically literate disciple of the Lord Jesus Christ—useful as a worker in your local church in reaching the lost with the gospel and training believers in discipleship.

The claims of discipleship include a call to commitment by men and women who want to follow Jesus. They grow as disciples by getting into the Word as a habit of life and applying it consistently to their daily lives.

George Mueller, the director of a series of orphanages in Bristol, England, during much of the 19th century, was known as a man of faith and prayer. It is amazing to read the answers to prayer this man had during his long life. What made him a man of faith and prayer? During his lifetime he read through the Bible over 200 times, and more than half of those readings he did on his knees, praying over the Word and studying it diligently.

When you know the Word of God that well, you are going to know the will of God for your life. When you know the will of God, you will be able to pray specifically and get specific answers.

If we were to ask in a church meeting, "How many of you *believe* the Bible from cover to cover?" probably everyone would raise a hand. However, if we were to ask, "How many of you *read it regularly* from cover to cover?" we might not get much of a response. It seems we are often guilty of being more interested in defending God's Word than in studying it.

On a typical evening an average Christian may sit and watch TV for three hours, but only read his Bible for three minutes before bedtime. Is it any wonder many lack spiritual maturity? Many Christians are more faithful to the Dear Abby column or the sports pages than they are to the Word of God. I have known non-Christians who would not leave their homes in the morning until they had read their horoscopes. What would happen if Christians committed themselves with equal vigor to reading their Bibles each morning before they left for work, school, or shopping? It would change their lives and the lives of those around them.

The apostle Paul said something important about the Scriptures. Writing to Timothy, he declared:

> But as for you, continue in what you have learned and have become convinced of, because you know those from whom you learned it, and how from infancy you have known the Holy Scriptures, which are able to make you wise for salvation through faith in Christ Jesus. All Scripture is God-breathed and is useful for teaching, rebuking, correcting and training in righteousness, so that the servant of God may be thoroughly equipped for every good work (2 Tim. 3:14–17).

Paul gives us two reasons why we should know the Scriptures. The first purpose is that we might come to know Jesus Christ and receive his salvation (v. 15). We learn about him and redemption through the Word. The second purpose of Scripture is to help us grow spiritually that we might be equipped for whatever God wants us to do (v. 17). The means to that growth are teaching (doctrine), rebuking, correcting, and training (v. 16). Teaching shows us the path on which we are to walk; rebuking shows us where we got off the path; correcting tells us how to get back on the path; and training in righteousness teaches how to stay on that path. This means that the Bible is the comprehensive guidebook for living the Christian life.

Near the end of Jesus' ministry, the Jewish leaders were trying to trick him with complicated questions about their Law. To one question the Sadducees had designed to try to trap him, Jesus replied, "You are in error because you do not know the Scriptures or the power of God" (Matt. 22:29). Jesus gives here the two basic reasons for false doctrine, or error. People get off base doctrinally because they know neither their Bibles nor the power of God. All error comes from these two things.

With the current rise and popularity of cults, false teachings, and nonbiblical philosophies, it is imperative that we Christians be grounded in the Word of God so that we can discern error from truth.

Why is it that most Christians do not study the Word of God? Probably many reasons could be given, but three seem to be most common. The first reason is that *people don't know how.* This was my situation for many years. I would go to a Bible conference, retreat, or revival and hear great preaching. I would often leave the meeting amazed at the scriptural insight the various speakers possessed. Then I would think, *Why didn't I see that?* and I would try to study on my own. But because no one had shown me how to study the Bible by myself, I was unable to do it and felt frustrated. I knew God wanted me to study his Word, so I committed myself to learning how and to teaching others how it could be done.

If I were to meet a starving man by the side of a river, lake, or ocean, I could do one of two things: I could get my fishing rod and catch him a fish, thus satisfying his hunger for a few hours; or I could teach him how to fish, thus satisfying his hunger for his lifetime. The second option is obviously the best way to help that man. In the same way, hungry Christians need to be taught how to feed themselves from the Word of God.

The second reason why people don't study their Bibles is that *they are not motivated.* This is because they have not experienced the joy that comes from personally discovering truths from the Word of God. Past efforts at Bible study have been unfruitful, so they have given up. They have become satisfied with getting all they need for their Christian lives from somebody else rather than finding it out on their own. At this point, I must warn you about this book: If you get serious about studying the Bible on your own, you will never again be satisfied with a mere secondhand knowledge of the Scriptures. Dr. Paul Little once compared personal Bible study to eating peanuts. Once you get started doing it, you're hooked! When you discover how good Bible study "tastes," you will find yourself going back for more and more. Personal Bible study can be habit-forming!

The third reason why people don't study the Scriptures is that *they are lazy.* Bible study is hard work, and there are no shortcuts to it. It is just like anything else in life that is truly worthwhile: it takes time, effort, concentration, and persistence. Most great truths of the Word of God do not lie on the surface; we have to dig for them. Just as gold might be found at the bottom of a mine or a pearl at the bottom of the sea, so the deeper truths of God must be searched out with great diligence.

Howard G. Hendricks, well-known conference speaker and Christian education expert, has spoken of three stages of attitudes toward Bible study:

- The "castor oil" stage—when we study the Bible because we know it is good for us, but it is not too enjoyable.
- The "cereal" stage—when our Bible study is dry and uninteresting, but we know it is nourishing.

- The "peaches and cream" stage — when we are really feasting on the Word of God.

In the Western world we live in a society that prefers to have other people do our thinking for us. That's why TV and other forms of entertainment, including professional sports, are so popular. We want to relax and be entertained without having to think or exert any effort. In Bible study, however, we have to learn some techniques, some methods, and then concentrate on digging out the messages God has for us.

The purpose of this book is to teach you how to dig out the riches of the Word of God for yourself. It will require some serious thinking, but we have tried to keep the procedures simple.

In each chapter you will be introduced to one of 12 basic methods of personal Bible study. For the sake of clarity, each chapter contains the same basic components, though the order varies:

1. A condensed outline of each method. This allows you to gain an overview of each method at a glance. You will find this helpful whenever you need to refer back to the sequence of steps in a certain method.
2. A short definition of the method.
3. A rationale for each method. This acquaints you with the benefits and limitations of each method.
4. The procedure for each method. This is explained in a simple step-by-step manner.
5. An example of each method (a completed form).
6. A blank form that you can use or copy for your own study.
7. Suggested possible passages or subjects to get you started on your own study.
8. Suggestions for further reading related to each method.

Because each chapter is independent of the others, you may skip around in reading the book, choosing to learn first the methods that interest you most. However, with the exception of the last one, these methods are presented *in order of their difficulty.* There is a logical progression through the book. As you move from chapter to chapter, you will be introduced to additional Bible study skills. For the best results, you should master each method in the order given before proceeding to the next. Chapter 1, "The Devotional Method," is *foundational*; you should read and understand it before attempting any other method. It will teach you how to write out a personal application from Scripture, which you will then use as a final step in most of the other methods.

I trust that this book will become a well-worn and used reference tool that will guide you in a lifetime of personal Bible study and in your teaching others to do the same.

INTRODUCTION:
HOW TO STUDY
THE BIBLE

PRINCIPLES OF DYNAMIC BIBLE STUDY

Dynamic Bible study does not require anything magical. Once you understand the basic principles, it is simple to do. Here are five general principles you will need to remember, regardless of the method of study you use.

1. *The secret of dynamic Bible study is knowing how to ask the right kinds of questions.* The 12 methods of Bible study presented in this book require your asking questions of the biblical text. The main difference in these methods is the types of questions you will ask. You will have different types of questions with each method. Asking questions is a skill that you can develop. As you grow in proficiency in Bible study, you will develop the art of asking questions. The more questions you ask about the text under study, the more you will get out of it.

You will realize that you can bombard the text with a limitless number of questions. One benefit of studying the Bible is that you will begin developing a more inquisitive mind. You will discover exciting insights you've overlooked in the past. It will seem as if you have been given a new pair of eyes! Suddenly, every time you pick up the Bible to study, new truths will leap out of the text.

2. *Dynamic Bible study involves writing down what you have observed and discovered.* You haven't really thought through a biblical text until you have put the thoughts gained from it into writing. You *cannot* study the Bible without writing something down. That is the difference between Bible reading and Bible study. In reading the Bible you simply read through a selected portion of Scripture, whereas in studying the Bible you take extensive notes. Dawson Trotman, founder of the Navigators, used to say, "Thoughts disentangle themselves when they pass through the lips and the fingertips." If you haven't put your observations down on paper, you haven't really thought about them.

This principle is true not only in Bible study but also in many other areas of the Christian life. One of the most profitable things you can do in your spiritual life is to start some kind of spiritual notebook in which you write down thoughts and insights God has given you.

Nowhere is note-taking more important than in your personal Bible study. If you really value the nuggets of truth that you discover, you will take notes on everything you dig out of the Scriptures. Even if you don't see anything in a particular verse, write *that* down. Each Bible study method in this book has a study form designed to be used with it so that you can write down various notes on what you study.

3. *The ultimate goal of dynamic Bible study is application, not just interpretation.* We do not want to settle for understanding alone; we want to apply the biblical principles to our daily living. Dwight L. Moody, a great evangelist and Christian educator of the late 19th century, used to say, "The Bible was not given to increase our knowledge, but to change our lives." It was given to change our character and bring it more into conformity with Jesus Christ. All of our efforts in Bible study are valueless if in the final analysis we do not change and become more like Jesus. We must "not merely listen to the word," but we are to "do what it says" (James 1:22).

It is possible to know the Word of God and not know the God of the Word. One of the tragedies of our time is that some of the world's best Bible scholars are also some of the poorest soul-winners. They have the time to dig for great gems of biblical truth, but they seem to forget that one of the mandates of Scripture is to go out and make disciples. When we apply God's Word in our lives, we will also become eager to carry out the Great Commission (Matt. 28:18–20).

One day a man asked me, "What is the best translation?" (He was referring, of course, to the best Bible version.)

I answered, "The best translation is when you translate the Word of God into your daily life."

He said, "But I've got my *Living Bible.*" (He still didn't get the picture.)

I replied, "You ought to *be* a living Bible! The Word made flesh ought to be visible in your life."

Some of the questions you ought to be asking yourself in your Bible study are: What attitude do I need to change as a result of this study? What do I need to start doing or stop doing? What things do I need to believe or stop believing? What relationships do I need to work on? What ministry should I be having with others? Our goal in all Bible studies is to know Jesus Christ and to become like him in our attitudes, our thoughts, our speech, our actions, and our values.

When the Word of God changes our lives and makes us more like Jesus, that's when we realize what the real purpose of life is, what true joy is, and what it means for God to change the world through us. The Great Commission is fulfilled and souls are won when we become Christlike and do his will.

One further thought here: When you begin studying the Word of God, don't go to it with the attitude of finding some truth that no one else has ever seen. Don't study it to find something with which to impress others. Just go to the Word to find out what it has to say *to you.* The real problem for most of us is not with interpreting difficult passages but with obeying the passages we do understand.

4. *Dynamic Bible study means that God's Word must be studied systematically.* A haphazard study of the Word of God is an insult to the sanctity of Scripture. It is a slap at the holiness of God, who gave us that Word. The "cafeteria" style, the "dip-or-skip" method, or the "what-are-we-going-to-find-today" approach will not produce the results God wants in our lives. What we need is a systematic, regular plan of study, whether we go through a book, study a word, analyze a person's character, study a chapter, or choose some other method.

We should not overlook any passage or section in the Bible. The Old Testament is just as much God's Word as is the New. Many people today do not know too much about the Old Testament. It may be embarrassing for some to get to heaven and have Zephaniah ask them, "How did you like my book?" Because "*all* Scripture is God-breathed" (2 Tim. 3:16), we need to study all of it systematically. (A plan for such a systematic study is suggested in appendix G.)

Studying the Bible is like being a good detective. A good Bible student basically follows the same procedure as a good sleuth. The first thing a detective does is to go out and look for clues. He doesn't say anything, interpret anything, or draw any conclusions, but he does look at all the details. He observes things that other people might normally overlook, because he is trained in observation. Second, he begins asking questions on the basis of what he has observed. Third, after intense observation and questioning, he starts putting the evidence together and interpreting what he has. Fourth, he compares and correlates, piecing together all the evidence he has collected to see how each fact relates to the others. Finally, he draws a conclusion and makes a decision on the basis of what he believes actually occurred and who was involved.

A serious Bible student follows these same basic steps in approaching the Word of God. The first step is *observing*: seeing the basic facts contained in the text under study. Next comes *asking* questions: discovering additional facts by more intense observation. Third is *interpreting*: analyzing what the text means. Fourth is *correlating* what you have discovered with other biblical truths you know; this involves cross-referencing verses and comparing Scripture with Scripture. The final step is drawing a conclusion: *applying* to your life in a practical way the truths you have studied. (I am grateful to William Lincoln for the helpful detective analogy. His book *Personal Bible Study* [Bethany House, 1975] is an excellent introduction to the inductive approach to Bible study.)

5. *In dynamic Bible study you will never exhaust the riches in any one passage of Scripture.* The psalmist declared, "To all perfection I see a limit, but your commands are boundless" (Ps. 119:96). You can dig and dig in Scripture, but you will never touch bottom. Solomon said, "If you look for it as for silver and search for it as for hidden treasure, then you will understand the fear of the LORD and find the knowledge of God" (Prov. 2:4–5). But God's silver lode is inexhaustible and the treasure is boundless.

For this reason you can study the same passage over and over again, dig into it, leave it for three or four months—and when you come back to it, there is much more to find. The key is this: *Stick with it!* Remember that there is no limit to the number of questions you can ask, no limit to the observations you can make, no limit to the applications you can make. So don't give up. The best attitude to have in Bible study is the one Jacob had when he wrestled with the angel and said, "I will not let you go unless you bless me" (Gen. 32:26).

Bible study has no shortcuts. It is hard work, but if you are diligent and patient, you will reap results in due time. Once you have felt the joy and satisfaction that come from finding a fantastic spiritual truth on your own and applying it to your life, you will realize that it was well worth the effort. So stick with it!

PREPARATION FOR DYNAMIC BIBLE STUDY

You do not just rush into Bible study. Good Bible study demands some preparation. Here are four things that are important to you if you are to receive the most benefit from your study.

1. *Schedule your Bible study time.* Set aside a specific amount of time to do Bible study each week. Decide how much time you want to spend on Bible study. Don't overdo it, but don't shortchange yourself, either. If you don't put study into your weekly schedule, you will never make time for it or it will be sporadic and shallow. *You must make time for Bible study.*

How often should you study the Bible? The answer will vary from person to person, but an important factor to keep in mind is the distinction between your quiet time and your Bible study time. You should have a quiet time every day. It is usually a short devotional period (10–30 minutes) in which you *read* the Bible, meditate for a few minutes on what you have read, and have a time of prayer. The purpose of your quiet time is to have fellowship with Jesus Christ. (See appendix A for instructions on how to have a quiet time.)

You should not try to do in-depth Bible study during your quiet time. In fact, nothing will kill your quiet time faster than engaging in serious Bible study during that devotional period. Just enjoy the presence of God and fellowship with him.

While it is better to have a 10-minute quiet time every day than just a one-hour period once a week, the exact opposite is true in Bible study. You cannot study the Bible effectively in a piecemeal fashion. It is better to block out larger periods of time (two to four hours) than to try to study a little bit every day. Then as you grow in your Bible study skills, you can spend additional time with it.

Probably the worst enemy of Bible study today in the Western world is television. Surveys show that the TV is on 7 hours, 40 minutes per day in the average American home. The average American watches more than 4 hours of TV each day—which packed together would be 61 days of TV viewing per year. By age 18 the average American child will have seen 200,000 acts of violence, including 16,000 murders. By age 65 the average American will have spent about 9½ years in front of the tube (*http://tvturnoff.org/images/facts&figs/fact sheets/FactsFigs.pdf*.)

If, on the other hand, a person went to Sunday school regularly from birth until age 65, he would only have had a total of four *months* of solid Bible teaching. Is it any wonder that there are so many weak Christians in Western society? We have to discipline ourselves and make specific time for Bible study, and not let anything get in its way.

You should study your Bible when you are at your best physically, emotionally, and intellectually, and when you can be undistracted and unhurried. Since you are either a "day person" or a "night person," you should pick the time when you are most alert. You should never try to study when you are tired or right after a large meal. Try to study when you are rested and wide awake.

2. *Keep a notebook.* As already stated, you cannot study the Bible without writing down things that you have observed. Each study method suggested in this book has a study form designed to go with it.

3. *Get the right tools.* With each method of study is a list of suggested reference tools you will need for your study. The first few methods require few or no tools, while the later ones require a number of them. You should consider making an investment in these reference tools and setting up a little personal reference library. It will be an investment you will use the rest of your life. You will find a discus-

sion of these in the next section, with suggestions for a basic and more advanced library.

4. *Spend a short time in prayer before each study.* First, ask the Lord to cleanse your life from all known sin and to fill you with the Holy Spirit, so you will be in fellowship with him during the study. This is the advantage of studying the Bible as compared with studying a textbook: you have direct communication with the Author himself. You have the privilege of studying not only the revelation, but also the Revealer. So make sure you are in fellowship with Christ before you study his Word. The apostle Paul said that if you are in the flesh, or carnal, you cannot understand spiritual truths (1 Cor. 2:10 – 3:4). You have to be in fellowship with the Lord in order to understand and apply his Word. As someone said, "We need to search our hearts before we search the Scriptures." We need to make sure our lives are right with God before we try to dig into his Word.

Second, pray that the Holy Spirit will guide you in your study. The best way to understand the Bible is to talk with its Author. Memorize Psalm 119:18 and use it before each study: "Open my eyes that I may see wonderful things in your law." Ask God to open your eyes to his Word. In the final analysis, unless God the Holy Spirit opens your eyes to see the truths in the Bible, all of your studying will be a wasted effort.

SELECTING THE RIGHT TOOLS FOR GOOD BIBLE STUDY

Probably one of the best-kept secrets in Christendom is the availability of practical Bible study helps. Many Christians are not aware of the many excellent reference tools currently available to make personal Bible study possible and exciting. This is comparable to a carpenter who sets out to build a house without knowing that a hammer and saw are available to him.

Pastors should acquaint their people with these books, for the devil delights in keeping them out of circulation. As long as Satan can keep Christians from studying their Bibles on their own, his work will be that much easier. A Christian who does not spend regular time each week in personal Bible study will be weak in resisting the devil's temptations. A practical way that pastors can "equip [God's] people for works of service" (Eph. 4:12) is to familiarize their people with these Bible study tools.

THE PURPOSE OF REFERENCE TOOLS

Christians living in the Western world have an abundance of helpful books that are designed to aid us in our personal Bible study, making use of the latest archaeological finds, word studies, and research of great Bible scholars. Bible study tools, however, are not meant to replace the Bible; rather, they help us in studying the Bible itself. Bible study is a skill we need to develop. Most skills require the use of some kinds of tools. Carpenters need their hammers and saws; artists need their brushes and paints; plumbers need their wrenches. Likewise, serious Bible students will want to take advantage of the available reference tools to help them search the Scriptures effectively. People who try to study the Bible systematically without using good tools will find their job tedious and difficult.

Some Christians hesitate to use references out of fear that they will become too dependent on them. Some say piously, "All I need is the Bible." True, but the tools suggested in this section are designed to help you get *into* the Bible. You should not be afraid of using reference tools, for most of these books represent the lifelong studies of dedicated servants of God. The insights they received from the Lord can enrich your Bible study immensely and provide information about people, places, and events that you would not find in the Bible alone.

THE TOOLS THEMSELVES

In this section we look at eight types of reference tools that are used in the Bible study methods presented and explained in this book.

1. *The study Bible.* Your first and most important tool is a good study Bible. Some Bibles are more adaptable to personal Bible study than others. A good study Bible should have print large enough for you to read for long periods of time without getting a headache from eyestrain. It should also have paper thick enough for you to make notes without the ink running through the paper to the next page. Wide margins are helpful because they allow room for making personal notations. Finally, a study Bible should have a good system of cross-references.

I recommend the New International Version (NIV) because exhaustive concordances and various study Bibles are available today in that version. The study Bibles include a general edition as well as versions designed for particular categories of people, such as men, women, teenagers, and people still in their spiritual search for God.

Study Bibles and concordances are also available in the King James Version (KJV), but that version's archaic language can be a handicap unless you keep a more recent translation such as the NIV at your side during your Bible study.

2. *Several recent translations.* In the past 50 years we have seen the production of many new translations of the Bible that use contemporary English. Though weaknesses exist in every translation, each one makes a unique contribution to a better understanding of the Bible. Many people who were previously not interested in the King James Version have begun to read and study the Bible in the more recent translations. The greatest benefit you can receive from these versions is comparing them one with another in your study. The many possible meanings and usages of a word can be found by reading a verse in the various versions and noting the differences.

Also available today are some "parallel" Bibles, which include several translations side by side in a single volume. This allows you to compare translations quickly without having to lay out 10 Bibles across your desk. Besides these recent translations, a few well-known paraphrases have been produced. A translation is more of a word-for-word translation from the original language; a paraphrase is what one person believes the original says, which calls for inclusion of their own interpretation in some places. Most translations have been prepared by a group of scholars, while a paraphrase is the work of one person. Paraphrases are fine for occasional light devotional reading, but should not be used for serious Bible study. Use an accurate and respected translation for that.

Some useful and reliable translations available today besides the NIV are

- *The New American Standard Bible* (produced by the Lockman Foundation and published by Zondervan and several other publishers), recognized as one of the most accurate translations that is faithful to the original languages.
- *The Amplified Bible* (produced by the Lockman Foundation and published by Zondervan), a translation that includes different possible meanings of many words used in the text. It seeks to show the many renderings a Greek or Hebrew word can have, so you can understand the full implications of its usage. (Some say it allows readers to select their own meanings.) It is helpful in doing word studies, but is not recommended as a regular reading Bible.
- *The New Living Translation* (produced and published by Tyndale House), a contemporary translation that has a dynamic approach to language similar to that of the NIV. It is a little freer in its language than the NIV, but it is not a paraphrase like its predecessor, *The Living Bible*.

Many other fine translations are available today, so choose the ones with which you will be most comfortable. Two or three different recent Bible translations will get you started.

Two paraphrases are *The Living Bible* by Kenneth Taylor (Tyndale) and *The Message* by Eugene Peterson (NavPress).

3. *An exhaustive concordance.* By far the most important tool you will need in Bible study next to your study Bible is a concordance geared to your primary Bible version. This tool is a Bible index of the words contained in that version. A number of Bibles have limited concordances at the back, which list only a few of the major words and names. An "exhaustive" concordance lists every usage of every word in the Bible and gives all the references where that word may be found.

Exhaustive concordances are available today for various versions of the Bible. They are the descendants, adapted to more recent translations, of the original *Strong's Exhaustive Concordance* (various publishers) that was compiled for the King James Version. Two of these are the following:

- *The Strongest NIV Exhaustive Concordance* (Zondervan)
- *The Strongest NASB Exhaustive Concordance* (Zondervan)

In addition, there is *Young's Analytical Concordance to the Bible* (Eerdmans), which, like Strong's, originated in the 19th century and is based on the King James Version. Young's is better than Strong's for word studies because of the way it is organized. All exhaustive concordances are large, bulky volumes that are fairly expensive, but they are worth every penny you invest in them.

You will need a concordance in all but two of the methods presented in this book.

4. *A Bible dictionary and/or Bible encyclopedia.* A Bible dictionary explains many of the words, topics, customs, and traditions in the Bible as well as giving historical, geographical, cultural, and archaeological information. Background material is also given for each book of the Bible, and

short biographies are presented for the major people of both testaments. A Bible encyclopedia is an expanded Bible dictionary, with longer articles that deal in greater detail with more subjects. Some of the best are

- *Baker Encyclopedia of the Bible*, 2 vols. (Baker)
- *The Complete Book of When and Where in the Bible* (Tyndale)
- *Holman Illustrated Bible Dictionary*, rev. ed. (Broadman & Holman)
- *The Illustrated Bible Dictionary*, 3 vols. (Tyndale)
- *Nelson's New Illustrated Bible Dictionary* (Nelson)
- *New Bible Dictionary*, 3rd ed. (InterVarsity Press)
- *Tyndale Bible Dictionary* (Tyndale)
- *The Zondervan Encyclopedia of the Bible*, 5 vols. (Zondervan)

5. *A topical Bible.* This tool is similar to a concordance except that it categorizes the verses of the Bible by topics instead of by words. This helps a Bible student because a verse often deals with a topic without ever using the specific word. If you had to rely on your concordance alone, you might miss those verses when studying a particular subject. For example, if you were to look up the subject "Trinity" in *Nave's Topical Bible,* you would find 83 references listed, even though the actual word does not appear in the Bible.

Another helpful feature is that the verses under each topic are written out in full, which allows you to scan the key verses on a topic quickly without having to look up each one in your Bible. You must note, however, that a topical Bible is not exhaustive, for not every verse related to a topic is necessarily listed.

The standard topical Bible for the King James Version is *Nave's Topical Bible* (Moody Press). Billy Graham has said that apart from his Bible, this is the book he uses more than any other. For a more contemporary version, see the *Zondervan NIV Nave's Topical Bible.*

6. *A Bible handbook.* This tool is a combination of an encyclopedia and a commentary in concise form. It is used for quick reference while reading through a particular book of the Bible. Instead of being arranged by topics alphabetically, handbooks are designed to follow the order of the books of the Bible. They give background notes and a brief running commentary and include maps, charts, archaeological notes, and many other helpful facts. The best ones are

- *Halley's Bible Handbook with the New International Version* (Zondervan)
- *Holman Bible Handbook* (Broadman & Holman)
- *The New Unger's Bible Handbook* (Moody Press)
- *Zondervan Handbook to the Bible*, 3rd ed. (Zondervan)

7. *A set of word studies.* This is one area where today's Christian has the great privilege of profiting from the work of Bible scholars. Because of the availability of practical reference tools written for the average Christian, you can now study the original words of the Bible without knowing anything about Hebrew or Greek. Some scholars have spent their lives searching out the full meanings of the original words, then writing about them in simple, comprehensible language.

A good set of word studies will give you the following information: the original root meaning of the Greek or Hebrew word (its etymology), the various uses of the word throughout the Bible and in similar nonbiblical literature of that historical period, and the frequency with which the word occurs in the Bible.

These reference tools range from inexpensive one-volume expository dictionaries to very expensive 12-volume sets. These four are recommended:

- *The Bible Knowledge Key Word Study: New Testament*, 3 vols. (Victor)

- *The Bible Knowledge Key Word Study: Old Testament*, 4 vols. (Victor)
- *Expository Dictionary of Bible Words* (Hendrickson)
- *Kregel Dictionary of the Bible and Theology* (Kregel)

8. *Commentaries.* A commentary is a scholarly collection of explanatory notes on and interpretations of the text of a particular Bible book or section. Its purpose is to explain and interpret the meaning of the biblical message by analyzing the words used, background, introduction, grammar and syntax, and relation of that particular book to the rest of the Bible. Used properly, commentaries can greatly increase your understanding of the Bible. Generally, you should not refer to a commentary until *after* you have done your own study. Don't let someone else rob you of the joy of discovering biblical insights on your own. Never let reading a commentary take the place of your personal Bible study.

Because commentaries are written by people, they are fallible. Sometimes equally able commentators disagree on interpretations of the same biblical text. The best way to use a commentary is to check your own findings with those of the authors/commentators and discover whether they are solid and evangelical in their commitment to Scripture. Beware of buying and using commentaries written by people who do not regard the Bible as the Word of God.

Commentaries come in all sizes, ranging from one volume covering the whole Bible to multivolume sets. Here are some good one-or-two-volume commentaries:

- *Baker Commentary on the Bible* (Baker)
- *Bible Knowledge Commentary*, 2 vols. (Victor)
- *Expositor's Bible Commentary: Abridged Edition*, 2 vols. (Zondervan)
- *Nelson's New Illustrated Bible Commentary* (Nelson)
- *New Bible Commentary: Twenty-First-Century Edition* (Inter-Varsity Press)

Commentary series with more volumes include the following. Some series are incomplete, with some volumes still to be published.

- *The Bible Exposition Commentary,* 4 vols. (Victor)
- *Cornerstone Biblical Commentary,* 18 vols. (Tyndale)
- *Expositor's Bible Commentary,* 13 vols. (Zondervan)
- *Holman New Testament Commentary* (Broadman & Holman)
- *Holman Old Testament Commentary* (Broadman & Holman)
- *New American Commentary,* 44 vols. (Broadman & Holman)
- *The NIV Application Commentary,* 20 vols. Old Testament, 20 vols. New Testament (Zondervan)

A BASIC LIBRARY

A person just beginning personal Bible study should obtain only the basic tools necessary to get started. For the Bible study methods presented in this book, the following compose a basic library:

1. A study Bible
2. Two recent Bible versions
3. An exhaustive concordance
4. A Bible dictionary
5. A topical Bible
6. A Bible handbook
7. A one-or-two-volume commentary

A MORE ADVANCED LIBRARY

As you become proficient in your personal Bible study and feel comfortable using the tools in your basic library, you might want to begin adding advanced tools to your collection. In addition to the above seven tools, the following are recommended:

1. Additional versions and paraphrases
2. A Bible encyclopedia
3. A set of word studies
4. Individual commentaries on Bible books
5. A Bible atlas
6. Old and New Testament surveys
7. Any additional books that interest you, perhaps some listed in the bibliography

CONCLUSION

At this stage you might be thinking, *That's a lot of books!* You are absolutely right, but think of them as long-term investments in your spiritual life. Many books you buy are read once, then put on the shelf to gather dust. But reference books are used over and over again as you study the Bible, and they can give a lifetime of enjoyment. If you are serious about personal Bible study, you will want to acquire these tools regardless of cost.

Start saving money to buy these tools, and begin with the basic library. If you will set a goal of buying one book a month, in a year's time you will have a respectable and valuable collection of reference tools. You might also consider asking for these as Christmas or birthday gifts. A book you use is a gift that lasts a lifetime.

Finally, encourage your church to set up a section of Bible study reference tools in its library. The church could purchase the more expensive tools, such as the encyclopedias, word studies, and commentary sets, then make them available to its members. In larger churches, the library could possibly obtain several copies of each tool.

Because the Bible is God's Word, Bible study must have a top priority. With these tools you will be able to dig into the Scriptures effectively, an all-important endeavor that will change your life.

PREVIEW OF
THE 12 BIBLE
STUDY METHODS

This book presents and explains 12 proven Bible study methods that will enable you to study the Bible on your own. They are given in the order of simplicity and use of reference tools, beginning with the easiest and moving on to the harder ones.

1. *The Devotional Method.* Select a short portion of your Bible and prayerfully meditate on it until the Holy Spirit shows you a way to apply the truth to your life. Write out a personal application.

2. *The Chapter Summary Method.* Read a chapter of a Bible book through at least five times; then write down a summary of the central thoughts you find in it.

3. *The Character Quality Method.* Choose a character quality you would like to work on in your life and study what the Bible says about it.

4. *The Thematic Method.* Select a Bible theme to study. Then think of three-to-five questions you'd like to have answered about that theme. Next, study all the references you can find on your theme and record the answers to your questions.

5. *The Biographical Method.* Select a Bible character and research all the verses about that person in order to study their life and characteristics. Make notes on their attitudes, strengths, and weaknesses. Then apply what you have learned to your own life.

6. *The Topical Method.* Collect and compare all the verses you can find on a particular topic. Organize your conclusions into an outline that you can share with another person.

7. *The Word Study Method.* Study the important words of the Bible. Find out how many times a word occurs in Scripture and how it is used. Find out the original meaning of the word.

8. *The Book Background Method.* Study how history, geography, culture, science, and politics affected what happened in Bible times. Use Bible reference books to increase your understanding of the Word.

9. *The Book Survey Method.* Survey an entire book of the Bible by reading it through several times to get a general overview of its subject matter. Study the background of the book and make notes on its contents.

10. *The Chapter Analysis Method.* Master the contents of a chapter of a book of the Bible by taking an in-depth look at each verse in that chapter. Take each verse apart word by word, observing every detail.

11. *The Book Synthesis Method.* Summarize the contents and main themes of a book of the Bible after you have read it through several times. Make an outline of the book. This method can be done after you have used the Book Survey Method and the Chapter Analysis Method on every chapter of that book.

12. *The Verse-by-Verse Analysis Method.* Select one passage of Scripture and examine it in detail by asking questions, finding cross-references, and paraphrasing each verse. Record a possible application of each verse you study.

1

THE DEVOTIONAL METHOD OF BIBLE STUDY

How to Apply Scripture to Life

As we have already seen in the introduction, the ultimate goal of all Bible study is *application,* not interpretation. Since God wants to change our lives through his Word, it is important to learn how to apply Scripture to our lives before learning any other methods of Bible study. In fact, the techniques you learn in this chapter will be used in each of the following study methods. Regardless of the method you choose to use, at the end of each study you will need to make practical steps of application concerning the things the Lord shows you. (In this book, every time we talk about *application,* refer back to this method for an explanation.)

When you use these techniques by themselves (and not with another method), it is called the "Devotional Method of Bible Study." This is the type of simple study that you can use in your quiet time.

DEFINITION

The Devotional Method of Bible Study involves taking a passage of the Bible, large or small, and prayerfully meditating on it until the Holy

Spirit shows you a way to apply its truth to your own life in a way that is personal, practical, possible, and provable. The goal is for you to take seriously the Word of God and "do what it says" (James 1:22).

WHY APPLICATION IS IMPORTANT

The Bible was given to us to show us how we can have a relationship with Almighty God and how we are to live our lives his way in this world. It was given to change our lives to become more like that of Jesus Christ. The apostle Paul declared that it is useful for teaching, rebuking, correcting, and training the believer in righteous living (2 Tim. 3:16).

The Bible is a practical book, for it is concerned with practical godly living. Bible study without personal application can be just an academic exercise with no spiritual value. The Bible was written to be applied to our lives. In his succinct way Howard Hendricks has said, "Interpretation without application is abortion!" We want to note here that application is necessary for our Christian lives, that it is hard work, and that good applications are possible if we follow some basic principles.

APPLICATION IS NECESSARY FOR OUR LIVES

Study of the Word of God should lead to its application in our lives, with the result that the Scriptures change us to conform more with the will of God.

1. *You can't really get to know the Word of God unless you apply it to your life.* During his ministry Jesus had a number of encounters with the religious leaders of his time. These were primarily the Pharisees, the acknowledged scholars of the day; the scribes, legal and religious experts in Jewish law; and the Sadducees, the liberalizing

element in Jewish society at that time. On one occasion the Sadducees, who did not believe in the resurrection from the dead, asked Jesus a trick question.

Jesus' answer is indeed interesting. He said to them, "You are in error because you do not know the Scriptures or the power of God" (Matt. 22:29). The Sadducees had an intellectual knowledge of the facts of the Jewish Scriptures (our Old Testament), but they did not apply these principles in a personal way.

You can be a walking Bible encyclopedia, with your head crammed full of biblical knowledge, but it won't do you any good if you don't apply it practically in daily living. If you study the Word of God without applying it to your life, you are no better off than the Pharisees and Sadducees of Jesus' day. You really don't know the Scriptures until you put them into practice.

2. *Studying the Word of God can be dangerous if you merely study it without applying it.* Bible study without application can be dangerous *because knowledge puffs up.* The apostle Paul stated, "Knowledge puffs up while love builds up" (1 Cor. 8:1). The Greek word translated "puffs up" contains the idea of being inflated with pride that in turn leads to arrogance. The Bible tells us that the devil knows the Word intellectually (see his temptation of Jesus—Matt. 4:1–11), and we

STEP ONE—*Pray for Insight on How to Apply the Passage*

STEP TWO—*Meditate on the Verse(s) You Have Chosen to Study*

STEP THREE—*Write Out an Application*

STEP FOUR—*Memorize a Key Verse from Your Study*

also know that he is puffed up with pride and is arrogant. When you correctly apply the Word of God to your life, you eliminate the danger of being puffed up with pride.

Bible study without application can be dangerous *because knowledge requires action.* What a man knows should find expression in what he does. James declared, "Do not merely listen to the word, and so deceive yourselves. Do what it says" (James 1:22). God's commands are not optional. He doesn't say, "Please won't you consider doing this?" He commands, "Do it!" And he expects us to obey.

In the Sermon on the Mount, Jesus compared an obedient disciple to a wise man: "Therefore everyone who hears these words of mine and puts them into practice [action] is like a wise man who built his house on the rock" (Matt. 7:24). When the trials of life came along, the wise man's life stood firm while the foolish man's—the one who did not practice what he knew—came crashing down (Matt. 7:25–27). Also, King David was known as a man after God's own heart because he applied the Word to his life and practiced what he knew. The psalmist wrote, "I have considered my ways and have turned my steps to your statutes. I will hasten and not delay to obey your commands" (Ps. 119:59–60). You, too, need to put what you know into action.

Bible study without application can be dangerous *because knowledge increases responsibility.* If you get serious about studying the Bible, you will be held more accountable than the average person, because with added knowledge comes added responsibility. James wrote, "If anyone, then, knows the good they ought to do and doesn't do it, it is sin for them" (James 4:17). With a deeper knowledge of the Scriptures comes a stronger judgment if you fail to apply them. When you start studying the Bible, God begins showing you areas of your life that need changing and calls you to greater responsibility. If you are not planning on applying the lessons you receive from your Bible study, it would be better for you not to study the Bible at all! You will just be heaping more judgment on yourself!

John Milton, a great Christian poet, is reputed to have said, "The end of all learning is to know God, and out of that knowledge to love and imitate Him." That sums up what we are talking about in applying our study of Scripture: we are to know God, love him, and then be like him.

APPLICATION IS HARD WORK

It would seem that applying the Bible would be fairly simple, but actually it is the hardest part of Bible study. Why is that? Application doesn't happen by accident. We have to plan for it, or it will never come about. Three things that make applying Scripture to our lives so difficult are that it requires thinking, the devil fights it viciously, and we naturally resist change.

1. *Application is hard work because it requires serious thinking.* Sometimes it takes a long period of meditation (concentrated, prayerful thinking) before we see a way to apply a truth of Scripture we have studied. Sometimes it may mean looking beneath a temporary rule to see a timeless principle in the text. Sometimes it means looking beyond a local custom to see a universal insight. All this takes time and concentration that we may be hesitant and reluctant to give.

2. *Application is hard work because Satan fights it viciously.* The devil's strongest attacks often come in your quiet time when you are trying to apply what you have studied. Satan knows that as long as you are content with merely having head knowledge of the Word, you are not much of a threat to his plans. But as soon as you get serious about making some changes in your life, he will fight you tooth and nail. He hates doers of the Word. He will let you study the Bible all you

desire as long as you don't ask yourself, "Now what am I going to do with all that I've learned?"

3. *Application is hard work because we naturally resist change.* Often we don't "feel" like changing, which is what true application requires. We live by our emotions rather than by our wills, for we are content to stay the way we are. We hear Christians saying they don't feel like studying the Bible or they don't feel like praying or they don't feel like witnessing. Feeling has nothing to do with living the Christian life, for feelings come and go. The key to spiritual maturity is to live for Jesus Christ not because we feel good, but because we know it is the right thing to do. I have discovered that if the only time I study the Bible, pray, or witness is when I *feel* like it, the devil makes sure I never feel like it!

You apply the Word of God to your life not because you may feel like it that day or week, but because you know God expects it of you. Applied Bible study as an act of the will leads to maturity and is a basis for stability in your Christian life.

FOUR STEPS TO PRACTICAL APPLICATION

When you do a devotional Bible study, follow four simple steps. These steps can be summarized in the words *pray, meditate, apply,* and *memorize.*

STEP ONE   *Pray for Insight on How to Apply the Passage*

Ask God to help you apply the Scripture you are studying and show you specifically what he wants you to do. You already know that God wants you to do two things: obey his Word and share it with others. In your prayer tell God that you are ready to obey what he will show you and that you are willing to share that application with others.

STEP TWO	*Meditate on the Verse(s) You Have Chosen to Study*

Meditation is the key to discovering how to apply Scripture to your life. Meditation is essentially thought digestion. You take a thought God gives you, put it in your mind, and think on it over and over again. Meditation may be compared to rumination; that's what a cow does when it chews its cud. It eats some grass and sends it to its first stomach; then it lies down, brings the grass up, chews on it, and swallows it again. This process of digestion is repeated three times. Scriptural meditation is reading a passage in the Bible, then concentrating on it in different ways. Here are several practical ways you can meditate on a passage of Scripture:

Visualize the scene of the narrative in your mind. Put yourself into the biblical situation and try to picture yourself as an active participant. Whether you are reading the historical books of the Old Testament, the Gospels, or the book of Acts, imagine yourself in that historical context. Ask yourself how you would feel if you were involved in that situation. What would you say? What would you do?

If you are studying John 4, for example, visualize yourself as being right there with Jesus, the woman at the well, the disciples, and the inhabitants of Sychar. How would you feel if *you* were the one whom Jesus asked for a drink of water at the well near Sychar? What would *your* emotions be if you were one of the disciples who witnessed this incident?

Another example of visualization in meditation is to imagine yourself as the apostle Paul in prison writing the letter we know as 2 Timothy. Picture yourself in that Roman jail, condemned to death and awaiting execution, and alone except for Luke. Feel the loneliness Paul must have felt, but also feel the triumph he must have felt as he wrote, "I have fought the good fight, I have finished the race, I have kept the faith" (2 Tim. 4:7). When you start visualizing a scene, Scripture comes tremendously alive to you.

Emphasize words in the passage under study. Read through a verse aloud several times, each time emphasizing a different word, and watch new meanings develop. For instance, if you are meditating on Philippians 4:13, you would emphasize the words as follows:

"*I* can do all this through him who gives me strength."
"I *CAN* do all this through him who gives me strength."
"I can *DO* all this through him who gives me strength."
"I can do *ALL THIS* through him who gives me strength."
"I can do all this *THROUGH* him who gives me strength."
"I can do all this through *HIM* who gives me strength."
"I can do all this through him *WHO* gives me strength."
"I can do all this through him who *GIVES* me strength."
"I can do all this through him who gives *ME* strength."
"I can do all this through him who gives me *STRENGTH.*"

You will get 10 different meanings from this verse as you go through and emphasize a different word each time.

Paraphrase the passage under study. Take the verse or passage you are studying and rephrase it in your own words. As you think on it, use contemporary words and phrases to express timeless biblical truths. *The Living Bible* and Eugene Peterson's *The Message* are two examples of paraphrases of Scripture.

Personalize the passage you are studying. This can be done by putting your name in place of the pronouns or nouns used in Scripture. For example, John 3:16 would read, "For God so loved *Rick Warren* that he gave his one and only Son, that if *Rick* believes in him *he* shall not perish but have eternal life."

Use the S-P-A-C-E P-E-T-S acrostic. This acrostic is a useful aid to meditation. Each letter represents a question that can help you apply the passage to your life. If you memorize the nine questions that this acrostic represents, you will have them available every time you want to meditate on a passage. This acrostic asks: Is there any . . .

- **S**in to confess? Do I need to make any restitution?
- **P**romise to claim? Is it a universal promise? Have I met the condition(s)?
- **A**ttitude to change? Am I willing to work on a negative attitude and begin building toward a positive one?
- **C**ommand to obey? Am I willing to do it no matter how I feel?
- **E**xample to follow? Is it a positive example for me to copy, or a negative one to avoid?
- **P**rayer to pray? Is there anything I need to pray back to God?
- **E**rror to avoid? Is there any problem that I should be alert to or beware of?
- **T**ruth to believe? What new things can I learn about God the Father, Jesus Christ, the Holy Spirit, or other biblical teachings?
- **S**omething to praise God for? Is there something here I can be thankful for?

Pray the verse or passage back to God. Put the passage under study into the first person singular, turn it into a prayer, and pray it back to God. The book of Psalms is a good example of this method of meditation. Bill Gothard has said that David memorized the law of God, then personalized it and gave it back to God in the Psalms.

An example of this method of meditation may be seen in the use of the first three verses of Psalm 23:

> Thank you, Lord, for being my Shepherd, and that I lack nothing.

> Thank you for making me lie down in green pastures, for
>   leading me beside quiet waters, for refreshing my soul.
> Thank you for guiding me along the right paths for your
>   name's sake.

Which one of these methods should you use in your meditation? The one that best fits what you are studying, or a combination of them. If you are studying the book of Proverbs, for example, it may be difficult to visualize a scene in your mind, but you can emphasize the words and pray some of the teachings back to God.

STEP THREE   *Write Out an Application*

Write an application of the insights you have discovered through your meditation. Writing your application out on paper helps you be specific. If you don't write something down, you will soon forget it. This is particularly necessary when you are dealing with a spiritual truth. If you can't put it down on paper, you haven't really thought it through. It's been proven that if you write something down, you will remember it longer and be able to express to others what you have learned.

You need to remember four factors in writing out a good application:

1. Your application should be *personal*—you should write it in the first person singular. Use the personal pronouns *I, me, my,* and *mine* throughout.
2. Your application should be *practical*—it ought to be something you can *do.* Plan a definite course of action that you intend to take. Design a personal project that will encourage you to be a "doer of the Word." Make your applications as specific as possible. Generalities can make you feel helpless and produce little action.

3. Your application should be *possible*—it should be something you know you can accomplish. Otherwise you will get discouraged.
4. Your application should be *provable*—you must set up some sort of follow-up to check up on your success in doing it. It has to be *measurable* so you will know that you have done it. This means you will have to set some kind of time limit on your application.

The following example of these four factors is taken from Ecclesiastes 6:7. The passage reads, "Everyone's toil is for their mouth, yet their appetite is never satisfied." The four factors in the written application would look as follows:

1. *Personal*: "I need to ..."
2. *Practical*: "I need to lose some weight."
3. *Possible*: "I need to lose 10 pounds."
4. *Provable*: "I need to lose 10 pounds before the end of the month."

To help you carry out this kind of application, tell a friend or someone in the family about it who will occasionally check up on your progress in an encouraging way.

Record applications for future use as well as present needs. What if you find an application that does not apply to you at that particular time? You are studying a passage that has to do with death and how you can overcome grief and sorrow, but this is not your problem now. What do you do with these verses? Write them down anyway, for two reasons. First, the application might be needed in the future when another situation comes into your life. Second, it might help you minister to someone else who is in that situation. Ask yourself, "How can I use this verse to help someone else?"

STEP FOUR   *Memorize a Key Verse from Your Study*

So that you can continue to meditate on the passage you are applying, and to help remind you of your project, memorize a verse that is a key to the application you have written.

Sometimes God will work on one area of your life for several weeks or even months. It takes time to change ingrained character traits, habits, and attitudes. New habits and ways of thinking are not set in one day. We must be aware of this and be willing to let God continue to reinforce a new truth in our lives. We should not fool ourselves by thinking that writing out one application will be a magic formula that will produce instant change. Rather, it must be thought of as part of the process of growth. The memorized verse will help in that process because it will ever be with us — "in the heart."

On one occasion my application was to work on the quality of sensitivity. It took several months for God to build that quality into my life. I needed to see how this quality related to all areas of my life. He kept putting me into situations where I was tempted to do the opposite — be insensitive. He may do the same with you. God may teach you to love others by putting you in the midst of unlovely people. You may have to learn patience while experiencing irritations, and learn peace in the midst of chaos. You are then discovering how to have joy even in times of sorrow and testing. You must realize that when God wants to build a positive quality in your life, he must allow you to encounter situations where you can choose to do the right thing instead of following your natural inclinations.

SUMMARY

The ultimate test by which we study and apply Scripture is the person of Jesus Christ. We have to ask, "Does this application help me become more like Jesus?"

A man saw his neighbor coming out of a church one Sunday morning. He asked the churchgoer, "Is the sermon done?"

The neighbor wisely replied, "No. It was preached, but it has yet to be done."

If we do not apply the biblical insights God gives us, we become spiritually hardened and callous. We become dull to the convicting work of the Holy Spirit in our lives. Application of God's Word is vitally necessary to our spiritual health and our growth in Christian maturity.

HOW TO FILL IN THE DEVOTIONAL STUDY FORM

At the end of this chapter is a Devotional Study Form that you may reproduce for using this method. Or you may use a blank sheet of paper on which you have marked off the suggested divisions.

Filling Out the Form

Fill in the preliminary information:

- Date: [Write down the date that you do this study.]
- Passage: [Write down the book, chapter, and verse(s) that you are studying.]

Fill in the four parts of the form:

- Prayer: Check the box after you have prayed for insight.
- Meditation: Write out your thoughts using whichever method you employ.
- Application: Write out an application that is personal, practical, possible, and provable.
- Memorization: Write out the memory verse you plan to learn, in the version of your choice.

Sample Filled-out Form

See the examples on the following pages.

Assignment

The following passages are suggested as beginning study texts for the Devotional Method.

- Psalm 15
- Psalm 34
- Romans 12
- 1 Thessalonians 5:12–22
- 1 John 4

For Further Reading

The following books and pamphlets are helpful aids for establishing a regular quiet time. They contain some practical information on developing a daily habit of spending time in a devotional study of God's Word.

Appointment with God by the Navigators (NavPress)

"How to Have a Meaningful Quiet Time" by Rick Warren (appendix A of this book)

Meditation: The Bible Tells You How by Jim Downing (NavPress)

A Primer on Meditation by Robert D. Foster (Challenge Books)

Seven Minutes with God by Robert D. Foster (Challenge Books)

Studying, Interpreting, and Applying the Bible by Walter A. Henrichsen and Gayle Jackson, chap. 13 (Zondervan)

———— DEVOTIONAL STUDY FORM ————

DATE: June 30   **PASSAGE:** Luke 12:22–26

1. PRAYER   □ **(check when done)**

2. MEDITATION   This is my personalized paraphrase.

I shouldn't worry so much. God will take care of all my needs. Since God gave me my life, surely I can trust him to sustain it. I can learn from the example of birds: they don't worry about the future. God takes care of them on *a daily* basis. And if God takes care of the birds, of course he will take care of me! Besides, worrying never does me any good. It never really changes the situation. So what's the use of worrying? None!

Command to Obey: *Don't worry!* (v. 22)

Promise to Claim: *God will take care of me!* (v. 24)

3. APPLICATION

I need to apply this lesson in the area of our family finances.

For this next month (I'll take it one month at a time), every time the devil tempts me to worry about our bills, I'll resist that thought by quoting Luke 12:24 *aloud.*

4. MEMORIZATION

"Consider the ravens: They do not sow or reap, they have no storeroom or barn; yet God feeds them. And how much more valuable you are than birds!" (Luke 12:24)

DEVOTIONAL STUDY FORM

DATE: July 10   **PASSAGE:** Judges 6:1–18

1. PRAYER   ☐ (check when done)

2. MEDITATION   This passage is on the call of Gideon.

Lessons (Truths to Believe)

- When God wants to accomplish something, he looks for people to use.
- God often uses the most unexpected people.
- God can show his strength best through our weaknesses.
- God's power in us is the answer to our inadequacies.

Sin to Confess/Attitude to Change

Lord, forgive me for not being willing to be used by you. I've felt that you couldn't use me because of my weaknesses. I've used my inadequacy as an excuse for laziness. Help me remember that trusting in myself will cause failure, but relying on your strength in me will bring victory. Use my weaknesses to bring glory to yourself.

3. APPLICATION

I've been afraid to accept my church's invitation to teach a Sunday school class. I've made up excuses for not taking the position because I felt inadequate. But I know God wants me to teach that class, so I'm going to tell my pastor I'll accept the responsibility.

4. MEMORIZATION

Remember what God told Gideon: "I will be with you" (v. 16).

DEVOTIONAL STUDY FORM

DATE: **PASSAGE:**

1. PRAYER   ☐ (check when done)

2. MEDITATION

3. APPLICATION

4. MEMORIZATION

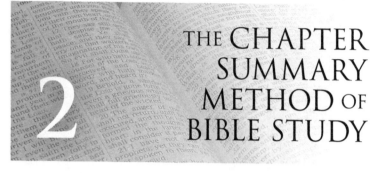

THE CHAPTER SUMMARY METHOD OF BIBLE STUDY

How to Begin Understanding Chapters of a Book of the Bible

The Bible as it was originally written had no chapter or verse divisions. In fact, it wasn't until A.D. 1228 that Bishop Stephen Langton added the chapter divisions. These were added to make the various sections of the Bible more accessible to the readers. Some of these divisions are arbitrary and interrupt the flow of a writer's message. Usually, however, they provide good breaking points that are helpful in Bible study.

According to these divisions, there are 1,189 chapters in the Bible. If you studied one chapter each day, you could read through the Scriptures in just over three years. If you summarized two chapters a day, you could finish in about 20 months. This pace is certainly not recommended, because you could quickly get bored with the study method. Instead, select random chapters of Scripture that you want to study and use the summary method on those passages; or use a different method for variety.

DEFINITION

The Chapter Summary Method of Bible Study involves gaining a general understanding of the contents of a chapter of the Bible by reading it through at least five times, asking a series of content questions, and summarizing the central thoughts of the passage. (This method should not be confused with the Book Survey and Chapter Analysis methods — chapters 9 and 10.)

WHY THIS METHOD IS IMPORTANT

This method is important because it enables you to begin understanding chapters of the books of the Bible. It is a popular method for those beginning Bible study because chapters are usually fairly short, and it does not require deep study to do a chapter summary. It is a valuable method because it can be quickly learned by a brand-new Christian or someone else who is interested in doing meaningful Bible study. It is an excellent method with which to begin a lifetime of personal Bible study for four reasons.

1. *This method is easy to learn.* You can begin practicing it as soon as you understand the 10 basic steps that follow in the next section. The study form and example at the end of this chapter should help you.

2. *This method does not take much time.* Depending on the length of the chapter you are studying, you can complete a chapter summary in 20 to 30 minutes. This is especially true if the chapter contains a historical narrative — parts of the Old Testament, the Gospels, and the book of Acts, for example. You will have to spend more time, however, in the Psalms, the prophetic books, and the doctrinal letters of the New Testament.

3. *This method does not require any outside helps or reference tools, but it is necessary to memorize the 10 steps.* Then you can do a

chapter summary in any situation at any time, using your Bible and a piece of paper. Whenever you have extra time to spend — as in a doctor's waiting room, a bus depot, or an airport — this is the method to use. Pick a book of the Bible, start with chapter 1, and begin recording your discoveries. I like to use this method when I go to a retreat and cannot take my reference tools with me.

4. *This method is a good type of study to use when you are engaged in a rapid reading survey through the Bible.* You can make initial notes as you read each chapter by using the Chapter Summary Form.

STEP ONE — *Caption*	**STEP SIX** — *Challenges*
STEP TWO — *Contents*	**STEP SEVEN** — *Cross-References*
STEP THREE — *Chief People*	**STEP EIGHT** — *Christ Seen*
STEP FOUR — *Choice Verse*	**STEP NINE** — *Central Lesson(s)*
STEP FIVE — *Crucial Word(s)*	**STEP TEN** — *Conclusion*

TEN EASY STEPS FOR DOING A CHAPTER SUMMARY

In preparing to fill in the study form for this method of Bible study, *read through the chapter at least five times.* You will find no better way to get acquainted with a chapter of the Bible than to read it over and over again. The more times you read a passage of Scripture, the more it will come alive to you. Many Christians miss the great insights of Scripture because they fail to read and reread its passages.

The great Bible expositor G. Campbell Morgan was famous for his powerful, exciting sermons. When asked for the secret of his ability to communicate God's Word, he replied that he made it a habit to read a chapter or passage 30 or 40 times before he began working on it for a sermon. It is no wonder his sermons were exciting and meaningful.

Here are some tips on how to read a chapter of the Bible:

- *Read it in a Bible without notes.* If you try using this method by reading a Bible in which you have made notes, you will have the tendency to concentrate on the same ideas. Let God speak to you in a fresh way and give you new insights.
- *Read it without stopping.* During your first few readings, don't stop in the middle of a chapter, but read it from start to finish. Your goal is to feel the flow of the chapter, so don't be concerned with the details at the outset. Try to capture the central message and the writer's overall theme.
- *Read it in several different contemporary translations.* This will give you additional insights as you see how each translator rendered the original writing. Make notes on the interesting differences you find.
- *Read it aloud quietly to yourself.* If you have a problem with concentration, this will help tremendously because you will be hearing yourself read. Many people have found that reading aloud helps them better focus their attention on the text.

As you are rereading the chapter, begin looking for the following 10 specific things and write your answers on your Chapter Summary Form or on a blank piece of paper. You may fill in the 10 Cs in any order, saving Step Ten for the last step. The 10 parts of your study are

aption
ontents
hief People
hoice Verse
rucial Word(s)
hallenges
ross-References
hrist Seen
entral Lesson(s)
onclusion

STEP ONE *Caption*

Give the chapter a short, descriptive title. The shorter the title, the more likely you will remember it. In fact, if you use this method on every chapter in a selected book of the Bible, you can remember the contents of the whole book by memorizing your chapter titles. Use one word if possible (1 Corinthians 13 might be titled "Love") and five words at most (Hebrews 11 could be "Heroes of the Faith"). Try to find the key word of the chapter and fit it into your title.

If your title is catchy or produces a mental picture, you will remember it longer. One creative person gave "Well-Well" as a title for John 4. The two key events of that chapter are the woman at the *well* and the nobleman's son whom Jesus made *well*.

STEP TWO *Contents*

Describe, summarize, paraphrase, outline, or make a list of the major points in a chapter. The method you choose will depend on the literary style of the chapter and on your own preference. Some people like to summarize; analytical people enjoy outlining. Choose the method with which you feel most comfortable and which is easy for you to do. Don't try to interpret the chapter; just make observations on its contents. Record on your form what you feel the writer said.

STEP THREE *Chief People*

List the most important people in the chapter. Ask questions such as, Who are the main people in this chapter? Why are they included? What is significant about them? If the chapter contains pronouns (*he, she, they,* etc.), you may have to refer to the previous chapter to identify the people. Write down your reasons for choosing certain people as the chief ones of the chapter. When you come to long genealogies (lists of people), don't try to list each one, but summarize the list.

STEP FOUR *Choice Verse*

Choose a verse that summarizes the whole chapter or one that speaks to you personally. In some chapters you may find a key verse that summarizes the writer's argument; in other chapters there may not be a key verse. On occasion you may want to pick a verse from which you will be writing your application, a verse that you believe God would have you apply to your life.

STEP FIVE *Crucial Word(s)*

Write down the key word or words of the chapter. Many times the key word will be the one that is used most frequently ("love" in 1 Corinthians 13 and "faith" in Hebrews 11). Sometimes the crucial word may be the most important word but not the most used one. In Romans 6, for example, the word "count" (KJV, "reckon") is the important word even though it is used only once (Rom. 6:11). Also, a chapter may have more than one crucial word.

STEP SIX *Challenges*

List any difficulties you may have with the passage. Are there any statements you do not understand? Is there any problem or question you would like to study further? Often while doing a chapter summary you will get ideas for other types of studies you may want to do in the future. For instance, a certain word in the chapter may catch your attention. Take note of that word; later you may want to do an in-depth study of it (see chap. 7). A question about a doctrinal matter might motivate you to do a topical study on that particular teaching (see chap. 6).

STEP SEVEN *Cross-References*

Using the cross-references in your study Bible, look up other verses that help clarify what the chapter is talking about and list them on your form. Ask the question, What else in the Bible helps me understand this chapter? Cross-references are important because they are helpful tools in interpreting the meaning of a chapter; they enable you to see what the Bible as a whole has to say on any given teaching. You can look for several types of cross-references, and these are described in the section on correlation in the Chapter Analysis Method (see chap. 10) and in chapter 10 of Walter A. Henrichsen and Gayle Jackson's book *Studying, Interpreting, and Applying the Bible* (Zondervan).

STEP EIGHT *Christ Seen*

The entire Bible is a revelation of the person of Jesus Christ. In fact, Jesus used the Old Testament to teach his disciples about himself. On the day of resurrection on the Emmaus road, Jesus taught two of his disciples: "Beginning with Moses and all the Prophets, he explained to them what was said in all the Scriptures concerning himself" (Luke 24:27). As you study each chapter, be alert for statements that tell you something about Jesus Christ, the Holy Spirit, or God the Father. Ask yourself, What can I learn about the nature of Jesus from this chapter? What attributes of God in Christ are illustrated here? (Some examples: his love, justice, mercy, holiness, power, and faithfulness.) This step may be the most difficult to complete in some portions of the Bible, particularly in Old Testament narratives and in passages where symbolism is used.

STEP NINE *Central Lesson(s)*

Write down the major principles, insights, and lessons you learn from this chapter. Ask yourself, Why does God want this passage in the Bible? What does he want to teach me from this chapter? What is the central thought the writer is trying to develop? A possible answer might be "We should be loving in all interpersonal relationships" (1 Cor. 13).

STEP TEN *Conclusion*

This is the *application* portion of your study. As discussed in chapter 1, develop a project to help you implement in your life a lesson you have learned from the chapter or portion. It will benefit you to conclude your chapter summary by asking yourself two questions: (1) How do these truths apply to me personally? and (2) What specifically am I going to do about them?

HOW TO FILL IN THE CHAPTER SUMMARY FORM

At the end of this chapter is a Chapter Summary Form that you can reproduce for your own use. The form has a place for listing the chapter of the Bible you are studying and the 10 steps of this method. Fill in the blank spaces for each of the 10 parts just described. If you need more room, use the back of the form or allow more room on your own paper.

Sample Filled-out Form

See the examples at the end of this chapter.

Assignment

Some chapters on which you can start using the Chapter Summary Method of Bible Study are

- 1 Corinthians 13
- 2 Timothy 2
- 1 John 1
- John 17
- The gospel of Luke (chapter by chapter)

For Further Reading

The Summarized Bible by Keith L. Brooks (Baker). This book is an excellent example of this method of Bible study. Dr. Brooks offers a chapter summary for every chapter of every book in the Bible and shows how Jesus Christ may be seen in each chapter. Don't read this book to help you do the study; only use it afterward to check to see how you have done on your own.

CHAPTER SUMMARY FORM

CHAPTER Luke 15   **Read 5 times ☐ (check when done)**

1. CAPTION (TITLE) Lost and Found

2. CONTENTS **This chapter contains three parables.**

1. Verses 3 – 7: The lost sheep
2. Verses 8 – 10: The lost coin
3. Verses 11 – 32: The lost son

3. CHIEF PEOPLE

The shepherd with the lost sheep
The woman with the lost coin
The father with the lost son

4. CHOICE VERSE

Luke 15:7 — "I tell you that in the same way there will be more rejoicing in heaven over one sinner who repents than over ninety-nine righteous persons who do not need to repent."

5. CRUCIAL WORD(S)

Lost (vv. 4, 8 – 9, 24, 32)
Found (5 – 6, 9, 24, 32)

6. CHALLENGES **(Difficulties I need to study)**

What does verse 7 mean — "ninety-nine righteous persons who do not need to repent"?

CHAPTER SUMMARY FORM

7. CROSS-REFERENCES Luke 15:4–6

Matthew 18:11–14	Isaiah 53:6
John 10:10–14	Psalm 119:176
1 Peter 2:25	

8. CHRIST SEEN

1st parable—Jesus the Good Shepherd searching for lost sheep.
2nd parable—the Holy Spirit our rightful Owner finding and restoring.
3rd parable—God the Father waiting to welcome us home.

9. CENTRAL LESSON(S)

Insights

The son went away saying, "Give me" (v. 12). He returned saying, "Make me" (v. 19). God cares for sinners and eagerly waits for them to return home.

Characteristics of the immature brother

Anger—v. 28
Childishness—v. 28
Jealousy—vv. 29–30
Wrong perspective—vv. 29–30
Grumbling—vv. 29–30

10. CONCLUSION   (Personal application)

In each of the three parables a concrete effort was made to recover what was lost. Many of my friends are lost without Christ. I need to develop specific witnessing plans for reaching them with the Good News. I will start by sharing my faith with my friend Jim this weekend.

I need to express more joy when I hear of people who have accepted Christ.

——— CHAPTER SUMMARY FORM ———

CHAPTER	**Read 5 times ☐ (check when done)**

1. CAPTION (TITLE)

2. CONTENTS

3. CHIEF PEOPLE

4. CHOICE VERSE

5. CRUCIAL WORD(S)

6. CHALLENGES **(Difficulties I need to study)**

CHAPTER SUMMARY FORM

7. CROSS-REFERENCES

8. CHRIST SEEN

9. CENTRAL LESSON(S)

10. CONCLUSION (Personal application)

3 THE CHARACTER QUALITY METHOD OF BIBLE STUDY

How to Determine Biblical Character Qualities

A major goal of Christian living is to develop Christlike character in our lives. Daily we want to become more and more like Jesus Christ by replacing bad character qualities with good ones. But before we can work on a Christlike quality in our lives, we must be able to recognize it. This study is designed to help you identify negative and positive character qualities and then be able to understand them.

You may then work on setting aside negative character qualities and building positive ones in your life. Doing these things will enable you to become more and more like Jesus Christ.

DEFINITION

The Character Quality Method of Bible Study involves finding out what the Bible says about a particular characteristic of a person, with a heavy emphasis on personal application. Furthermore, it is a combination in simplified form of three other Bible study methods: the Word Study Method, the Biographical Method, and the Cross-Reference Method.

It differs from the Biographical Method in that here you are studying the characteristics of a person rather than the person himself. These qualities can be negative or positive or both. The point is that we learn to avoid the negative ones and work on building the positive ones into our lives.

WHY THIS METHOD IS VITAL FOR OUR LIVES

The purpose of this method of Bible study is to *identify* character qualities taught in the Bible with the view of learning to avoid the negative ones and learning to work on the positive ones, so that we become more like the Lord Jesus Christ. It is obvious that until we know what a character quality is, we cannot avoid it or develop it. For example, if we wanted to become meek, as the Bible admonishes us to be, we would have to know what meekness is before we can really study it.

This is the first method in this book that requires the use of some tools. So let us look at some of the reference tools you will need:

1. A study Bible
2. An exhaustive concordance
3. A Bible dictionary and/or a word study book
4. A topical Bible
5. An English dictionary

If you want to develop positive biblical character qualities in your life, follow these tips:

1. Only work on one quality at a time. Don't try to work on two or three or more, for it takes concentrated effort to see how that one quality applies to every area of your life. It is far better to build one quality solidly into your life than to work on several weak ones.

2. Don't rush it! Character development takes time. Even though one of the steps is writing out an illustration after one week, you should probably want to work on one quality for a much longer time. I have found in my own life that God works on an area for months (sometimes years) before it becomes part of my daily walk with him.

3. Stay with that one quality until you get victory in that specific area. Don't skip around, trying to work on many qualities, when you need victory in that one. Remember that the quality of diligence is one you want to work on.

STEP ONE—*Name the Quality*

STEP TWO—*Name the Opposite Quality*

STEP THREE—*Do a Simple Word Study*

STEP FOUR—*Find Some Cross-References*

STEP FIVE—*Do a Brief Biographical Study*

STEP SIX—*Find a Memory Verse*

STEP SEVEN—*Select a Situation or Relationship to Work On*

STEP EIGHT—*Plan a Specific Project*

STEP NINE—*Write Out a Personal Illustration*

4. Be alert to a negative quality in your life that is actually a positive one being misused. Realize that the Lord wants to turn your weak points into strong ones. If you are rigid, legalistic, and unbending, it might be that the quality of self-discipline is being misused. That discipline needs to be tempered with compassion and concern for others.

5. Trust the Holy Spirit to build these qualities in your life. In the final analysis, it is God's power in you that reproduces the fruit of the Spirit in your life. It is God alone who can change your character. "For it is God who works in you to will and to act in order to fulfill his good purpose" (Phil. 2:13). So let God do it, trusting the Holy Spirit to work in your life.

NINE STEPS FOR DOING A CHARACTER QUALITY STUDY

STEP ONE *Name the Quality*

Select the quality you want to study and write it down. Then look it up in an English dictionary and jot down the definition of that word or concept. List any synonyms or related words that help you understand this quality.

STEP TWO *Name the Opposite Quality*

Write down the opposite quality—the antonym—of the one you are studying, and write out its dictionary definition and similar words. If you can't think of the opposite, use a dictionary of antonyms; some thesauruses also give antonyms. For example, *unfaithfulness* is the opposite of *faithfulness*. But for some qualities you might be studying, there might be two or more opposites. For example, you could have the following:

- Faith and doubt
- Faith and apathy
- Faith and fear

STEP THREE *Do a Simple Word Study*

Look up the Bible definition of the quality you are studying. Find the ways it is used in the scriptural contexts; then check a Bible diction-ary, encyclopedia, or word study book for the way the quality was used in biblical times and in the Scriptures. Some of the tools will tell you how many times the word is used in the Bible, each Testament, the writings of different authors, and the book you are studying.

For example, if you were studying the quality of meekness, you would discover that the word *meek* in the original Greek meant "breaking something and bringing it under submission." The word was used to describe the training of valuable horses, which were brought under submission to their masters. A stallion would still have all the power and strength of its wild days, but it was now under its master's control. Meekness, therefore, is not weakness. As a Chris-tian character quality, meekness is strength that is in submission to Jesus Christ.

STEP FOUR *Find Some Cross-References*

Using cross-references will give you additional insights from other portions of the Bible. Scripture is still the best interpreter of Scripture. Use your concordance and topical Bible to find all the verses you can relating to this quality. Look up the word and its synonyms in the concordance and topical Bible, write the cross-reference on the form in the appropriate section, and give a brief description of that verse. Then ask some of the following questions about the quality you are studying as you meditate on the cross-reference verses:

- What are the benefits this trait can bring me?
- What are some bad consequences this trait can bring me?
- What are benefits this trait can bring to others?
- What are some bad consequences this trait can bring to others?
- Is there any promise from God related to this trait?
- Is there any warning or judgment related to this trait?
- Is there a command related to this trait?
- What factors produce this trait?
- Did Jesus have anything to say about this quality? What?
- What writer talked about this quality the most?
- Is this trait symbolized by anything in Scripture? Is that significant?
- Is this trait listed with a group of qualities? What is the relationship between them? What does this suggest?
- What Scriptures tell me directly what God thinks of this trait?
- Do I want more or less of this trait in my life?

After asking a series of questions such as these, or others that you think of, you might write a brief summary of the Bible's teaching on this quality. You may list any lessons or principles that you learned from this mini-topical study, or you may paraphrase a few key verses on this trait.

Always be sure to write down any difficulties you have with the verses you looked up, or questions you would like to see answered. Possibly, later on you will understand what is difficult at present and then find answers to your problems; often one verse sheds light on another verse you have studied.

STEP FIVE   *Do a Brief Biographical Study*

Now go back to your Bible and try to find at least one person (more if possible) who showed this character quality in his or her life. Briefly describe this quality and write down the Scriptures that refer to it. Ask these questions as you do this part of the study:

- What shows this quality in his/her life?
- How did this quality affect his/her life?
- Did the quality help or hinder his/her growth to maturity? How?
- What results did it produce in his/her life?

An example of this step may be seen in the life of Joseph, the son of Jacob, who displayed different qualities of the fruit of the Spirit (Gal. 5:22–23) in each incident in his life. It is interesting to note his testimony before the heathen: "So Pharaoh asked them, 'Can we find anyone like this man, one in whom is the spirit of God?'" (Gen. 41:38). We find these qualities in Joseph:

- He displayed *love* in a difficult family situation (Gen. 47).
- He displayed *self-control* in a difficult temptation (Gen. 39).
- He displayed industry and patience in difficult circumstances (Gen. 39:19–40:23).
- He displayed *faithfulness* in a difficult task (Gen. 41:37–57).
- He displayed *goodness, gentleness,* and *kindness* in difficult family reunions (Gen. 42; 50).

Occasionally some of the qualities the Bible teaches are evident in the ways of certain animals (particularly in the book of Proverbs). When you find these qualities, write them down.

STEP SIX   *Find a Memory Verse*

Write down at least one verse from your cross-reference or biographical portion of the study that really speaks to you and that you intend to memorize during the following week. This verse should come in handy when God provides an opportunity for you to work on this character quality in a specific way.

STEP SEVEN   *Select a Situation or Relationship to Work On*

We are now getting to the application part of the study. Think of an area in your life in which God wants you to work on this character quality—avoiding it if it's negative or building it up if it's positive. This can be either a situation or an interpersonal relationship.

If it is a situation, anticipate in advance what you will do when the situation arises. Suppose you have been slothful, lazy. Your study on slothfulness has challenged you to get rid of this quality in your life. As you plan ahead, you know when situations will arise that will bring out the lazy streak in you, so you decide ahead of time what you will do: You will set *two* alarm clocks, one on the far side of the room, to help you get up in the morning to have a quiet time and be on time to work or school.

If it is a relationship, determine ahead of time how you will respond in your interactions with that person. This person could be your wife, husband, parents, children, girlfriend, boyfriend, work associates, school friends, or neighbors. Look for opportunities to work on that character quality in your relationship with that person or persons. Your goal is to have more mature relationships.

One way of doing this is to think back and recall a good situation or relationship in your recent past when you did work on this quality.

STEP EIGHT   *Plan a Specific Project*

This is the practical part of your application and is the actual working out of Step Seven. Think of a project that you will work on to build a positive quality in your life or to get rid of a negative quality.

Once I was working on the trait of gratefulness. One of my projects was to write grateful letters to five people who had been a blessing to me, saying, "I am grateful for you because...." Remember: applications should be personal, practical, possible, and measurable.

STEP NINE   *Write Out a Personal Illustration*

A few days after you have completed the first eight steps of this study, write out an illustration of how you were able to work on this quality. This is the "provable" (measurable) part of your application. Be specific, and write down where you have succeeded and where you might have failed. In just a short time you should be able to develop a whole set of personal examples of how God is working in your life, getting rid of negative qualities and building positive ones.

These illustrations serve a number of purposes. When you get discouraged, read over the backlog of your illustrations and see how God has worked in you. When you are working with a "Timothy," use your illustrations to teach him and to encourage him in his own illustrations. When you are sharing your testimony or teaching a class, use these illustrations to add a personal element to your presentation: "Here is how God worked in my life."

God often builds character in our lives by putting us in situations where we are tempted to do the opposite of what we should. For example, God may teach you honesty by placing you in a situation where you are tempted to be dishonest.

SUMMARY AND CONCLUSION

When I was in college, I was active in a musical group. I owned about $2,000 worth of the equipment it used. Once, when I was preaching 500 miles away, another music group at our school came to my roommate and asked if they could borrow my equipment. He told them, "I'm sure it would be all right, but you have to ask Rick first. I'm sure he will let you use it."

But because I was away, they didn't ask me. They simply came back after my roommate had gone and took the equipment. Later that weekend I called in and was told about my equipment being taken. I

73

got furious. I hung up the phone and was really steamed. I would have loaned it to them had they asked me, but they hadn't, and this was like stealing. I was upset, planning all kinds of things I would say and do when I returned.

In the meantime I had been doing a character quality study on forgiveness. That morning I had read in the Bible, "Make sure that nobody pays back wrong for wrong, but always strive to do what is good for each other and for everyone else. Rejoice always, pray continually, give thanks in all circumstances, for this is God's will for you in Christ Jesus" (1 Thess. 5:15–18). I suddenly realized that if I were to develop the quality of forgiveness, I had to forgive those people who had taken my equipment, I had to remain joyful, and I had to give thanks for the situation.

So here was a concrete situation that God had brought into my life that was going to help me build the character quality of forgiveness into my practical daily living. It was a tough lesson, but it was part of applying what we learn in Scripture. Writing that down has enabled me to share that experience with others.

HOW TO FILL IN THE CHARACTER QUALITY STUDY FORM

Use the form at the end of this chapter to write down the nine steps of your Bible study.

Sample Filled-out Form

See the example at the end of this chapter.

Assignment

A good place to start this study would be to go through the lists of qualities found in New Testament passages. Some positive ones are

- Matthew 5:3–12—the Beatitudes
- Galatians 5:22–23—the fruit of the Spirit
- Philippians 4:4–9—admirable qualities
- 2 Peter 1:5–8—qualities that should increase in our lives

Don't forget to study negative qualities as well, so that you can work on ridding these features from your life. Here are some negative qualities:

- Galatians 5:19–21—a list of the works of the flesh
- 2 Timothy 3:1–5—have nothing to do with these!

Below is a list of specific qualities taught throughout the Bible that you should study and work on.

Positive Qualities

1. Servanthood	7. Availability	13. Cooperativeness
2. Honesty	8. Teachability	14. Discipline
3. Humility	9. Forgiveness	15. Sincerity
4. Determination	10. Generosity	16. Contentment
5. Diligence	11. Loyalty	
6. Faithfulness	12. Fairness	

Negative Qualities

1. Laziness	7. Rebelliousness	13. Fearfulness
2. A critical spirit	8. Gossip	14. Lustfulness
3. Pride	9. Being unloving	15. Bitterness
4. Selfishness	10. Dishonesty	16. Apathy
5. Unfaithfulness	11. Impatience	
6. Disrespectfulness	12. Worry	

Many others may be found in Scripture, but these should get you started. A much longer list of biblical qualities, both negative and positive, is provided in appendix C.

For Further Reading

The Building of Character by J. R. Miller (AMG Publishers)
Character Sketches, 2 vols. (Institute of Basic Life Principles)
The Master Bible, edited by J. Wesley Dickson (J. Wesley Dickson & Co.)
The Measure of a Man by Gene Getz (Regal Books)
The Measure of a Woman by Gene Getz (Regal Books)

CHARACTER QUALITY STUDY FORM

1. CHARACTER QUALITY Boldness

"An exhibition of courage and fearlessness; bravery; willingness to move ahead confidently in the face of danger."

2. OPPOSITE QUALITY Timidity, Fearfulness

"To shrink back from a difficult or dangerous circumstance; to be hesitant."

3. SIMPLE WORD STUDY

Old Testament word:
Bâtah means "to be confident."
Example: Proverbs 28:1 — "The righteous are as *bold* as a lion."

New Testament words:
Tharreo means "to be confident, bold, or daring."
Example: Hebrews 13:6 — "So that we may *boldly* say, The Lord is my helper, and I will not fear what man shall do unto me" (KJV).

Parrçsiazomai means "to speak boldly or freely."
Example: Acts 19:8 — "Paul entered the synagogue and *spoke boldly* there for three months, arguing persuasively about the kingdom of God."

Reference tools used:

- *Young's Analytical Concordance to the Bible*
- *Vine's Expository Dictionary of New Testament Words*

——— CHARACTER QUALITY STUDY FORM ———

4. CROSS-REFERENCE INSIGHTS

- Christ spoke boldly in the face of opposition (John 7:26).
- Our confidence and boldness come from knowing that the Lord will help us in difficult situations (Hebrews 13:6).
- Peter and John were bold because they had been with Jesus (Acts 4:13).
- When the Holy Spirit fills our life, we will be able to speak the Word of God boldly. The first Christians prayed for boldness in witnessing and God answered their prayer by filling them with the Holy Spirit (Acts 4:29–31).
- When Christ's love is in us, we will be bold because there is no fear in love. Perfect love casts out all fear (1 John 4:17–18).

CHARACTER QUALITY STUDY FORM

5. SIMPLE BIOGRAPHICAL STUDY

The apostle Paul is a major example of boldness. His entire life seemed to be characterized by this quality:

- As a young Christian in Damascus, he witnessed boldly for Christ (Acts 9:27).
- Everywhere he went, he shared his faith boldly in spite of opposition and persecution:
  - ▸ in Jerusalem (Acts 9:28–29)
  - ▸ in Pisidian Antioch (Acts 13:46)
  - ▸ in Iconium (Acts 14:3)
  - ▸ in Ephesus (Acts 19:8)
  - ▸ in Thessalonica (1 Thess. 2:2)
- He wrote bold letters to the churches (Rom. 15:15).
- He asked people to pray that he would continually preach and teach with boldness (Eph. 6:19–20).
- His Christian testimony while in prison caused others to speak boldly for Christ (Phil. 1:14).
- He even faced death boldly: "According to my earnest expectation and hope, that I will not be put to shame in anything, but that with all boldness, Christ will even now, as always, be exalted in my body, whether by life or by death" (Phil. 1:20 NASB).

6. MEMORY VERSE(S)

"So we say with confidence, 'The Lord is my helper; I will not be afraid. What can mere mortals do to me?'" (Heb. 13:6).

——— CHARACTER QUALITY STUDY FORM ———

7. A SITUATION OR RELATIONSHIP
(where God wants to work on this quality in my life)

I have been afraid to witness to my friend Ted, who works with me at the office.

8. MY PROJECT

First, I will ask my wife to pray with me about overcoming my timidity in witnessing to Ted. Then, each day this week I will pause before going into the office and ask the Holy Spirit to fill my life and give me boldness to witness to Ted (Acts 4:31).

9. PERSONAL ILLUSTRATION

Monday and Tuesday of this week I prayed for boldness to witness to Ted, but the opportunity just didn't arise. Tuesday night I decided that I needed to be more earnest in my prayers, so I asked my wife to pray with me specifically for a chance to share my faith with Ted on Wednesday.

Wednesday morning, I paused at the office door before going in, and I prayed silently that Ted would sense that I "had been with Jesus," like Peter and John (Acts 4:13). Then I went in and placed my Bible on top of my desk, hoping Ted would recognize it.

During the coffee break, Ted came over to talk to me. He noticed my Bible and said, "Is that a Bible?"

I answered, "It sure is. Have you ever read it?"

"Not lately," he said.

I said, "Well I've been reading it a lot lately, and I've discovered some neat things in it." I then shared a brief testimony of what God was doing in my life. Ted seemed mildly interested—at least he wasn't turned off. It's a start, and I thank God for giving me the boldness to go this far.

CHARACTER QUALITY STUDY FORM

1. CHARACTER QUALITY

2. OPPOSITE QUALITY

3. SIMPLE WORD STUDY

─── CHARACTER QUALITY STUDY FORM ───

4. CROSS-REFERENCE INSIGHTS

──── CHARACTER QUALITY STUDY FORM ────

5. SIMPLE BIOGRAPHICAL STUDY

6. MEMORY VERSE(S)

RICK WARREN'S BIBLE STUDY METHODS

———— CHARACTER QUALITY STUDY FORM ————

7. A SITUATION OR RELATIONSHIP
(where God wants to work on this quality in my life)

8. MY PROJECT

9. PERSONAL ILLUSTRATION

4 THE THEMATIC METHOD OF BIBLE STUDY

How to Investigate Themes in Scripture

In the introduction to this book we noted that the secret of good Bible study is learning to ask the right questions. In doing a thematic study, you decide on a set of questions to ask about the chosen theme *before* you look in the Bible. Your questions should be based around what Rudyard Kipling called his "honest serving men" in his short story "The Elephant's Child."

> I keep six honest serving men:
> (They taught me all I knew)
> Their names are What and Why and When
> And How and Where and Who.

Use Kipling's serving men as you prepare the vital observation questions you want to ask in your thematic study: What? Why? When? How? Where? Who?

DEFINITION

The Thematic Method of Bible Study involves approaching a biblical theme with a set of not more than five predetermined questions in mind. You then trace that theme through the Bible or a single book by asking only those questions, summarizing your conclusions, and writing out a personal application.

The thematic study is similar to the topical study (see chap. 6), but differs in two ways. First, the thematic study is shorter than the topical because you study fewer verses. It is, in fact, a limited type of topical study. A topic may have many themes running through it. For example, one topic could be "Prayer," but you could study the following themes under that topic: "The Prayers of Jesus," "The Prayers of New Testament Writers," "Conditions for Answered Prayer," "Prayer Promises," "Intercession for Others," and many other prayer themes. A topical study would examine every possible verse that relates to the overall topic. In a thematic study you concentrate only on passages of Scripture that deal with your selected theme.

Second, a thematic study entails fewer questions. In a topical study you ask as many questions as you can, because your goal is to discover as much as possible about the topic. The thematic study has a limit of five carefully chosen questions. After making a list of all the verses related to the theme, you examine each verse by using only the questions you have prepared.

The reason for limiting the number of questions is that a theme may have 100, 200, or more references. If your set of questions gets too long, you will get bogged down and discouraged. You will get tired of the study even before you have finished it.

One week my wife decided to do a thematic study on the expression "the hand of the Lord." In her topical Bible she found only seven verses using that phrase, and in her exhaustive concordance she discovered a total of 210 references to the theme, under the word *hand*. She would have had her hands full if she had chosen to ask 15 or 20 questions of each verse.

WHY THIS METHOD OF BIBLE STUDY

The purpose of this method is to discover what you can about a chosen theme with specific, prepared questions that you will ask of each verse chosen for study. There are some great advantages in using it, and we will look at some practical tips for it.

TOOLS YOU WILL NEED

A few reference tools are needed for this method of Bible study:

- A study Bible
- An exhaustive concordance
- A topical Bible

ADVANTAGES OF THIS STUDY

Several advantages emerge from this method of Bible study:

1. You don't need many reference tools. You can do a limited study if you have only a topical Bible. But a topical Bible does not list all the references on a particular theme, so you will benefit by using an exhaustive concordance. You can make a list of every word that relates to the theme, then look up each word in the concordance and select the verses that deal specifically with your theme.

2. You can use this method when you don't have the time to do a full-scale topical study because the subject is too broad or because of the large number of Bible references on the subject.

3. This method is a good way to preview a topic by surveying the high points of its subordinate themes before attempting a regular topical study of the subject. Or you can use this approach when you are only interested in having certain questions answered on the theme. With this method you can discover exactly what you want to find out without spending valuable time on unrelated matters.

STEP ONE — *Choose a Theme to Study*

STEP TWO — *Decide on the Questions You Will Ask*

STEP THREE — *List All the Verses You Intend to Study*

STEP FOUR — *Ask Your Questions of Each Reference*

STEP FIVE — *Draw Some Conclusions from Your Study*

STEP SIX — *Write out a Personal Application*

4. This method is one of the easiest types of personal Bible study to turn into a sermon or Sunday school lesson. After completing your personal study, make each of your questions a major point in your talk and share the biblical answers with your group, class, or congregation.

5. This method is a good one for teaching your "Timothy" or any new Christian. It is simple enough for someone who has not yet done any personal Bible study to grasp and do effectively.

SOME TIPS ON DOING THIS STUDY

Because of the simplicity of the study and the danger of "getting carried away," some tips and words of caution are necessary.

1. Don't use too many questions. Even a theme under a major topic may be so vast as to have hundreds of Scripture references. If you list too many questions, you will not be able to do the study effectively. On a *major* thematic study you should ask no more than three questions.

2. Sometimes you can do a thematic study with only *one* question. Here are some examples:

- What are the things God hates?
- According to the New Testament, what things should we "endure"?
- What are the things we should "consider" as Christians?
- What traits of a fool are given in the book of Proverbs?
- According to Solomon (in Proverbs), what brings poverty?

3. Many times you will *not* find the answer to every one of your questions in the same verse. When that happens, just leave a blank space on your form and go on to the next question.

4. If you are not finding answers to *any* of your questions in your verses, it probably means you need to revise your questions. You may be asking the wrong ones. Possibly you are asking questions that God does not care to answer. Check the verses to see what God is really saying, and fit your questions to what he wants to tell you in those passages.

5. If you want to know *everything* God has said about a certain subject in the Bible, you will have to use an exhaustive concordance and look up all the words related to your theme. This can become a massive project. Remember that topical Bibles are not exhaustive, and you will have to use either a Young's or Strong's concordance.

SIMPLE STEPS ON DOING A THEMATIC STUDY

In doing a thematic study you will create some questions before looking up your references. These should include some of the six great investigative relative pronouns mentioned earlier. These words, when used in various combinations, will give you a limitless number of questions to use in your personal Bible study. For example, if you were to do a study on "Anger in the Book of Proverbs," you could ask such questions as these:

- What are the characteristics of an angry person?
- What causes anger?
- What are the results of anger?
- What is the cure for anger?

All four of these questions use the term "What?" but you could come up with just as many questions using the other five terms: Why? When? How? Where? Who?

STEP ONE   *Choose a Theme to Study*

Select a theme in which you are interested. If this is your first study of this kind, start with one that is small or short. In the Assignment section are some suggestions, including the questions; the example gives you a completed study.

STEP TWO   *List All the Verses You Intend to Study*

Using your three tools—the study Bible, the exhaustive concordance, the topical Bible—make a list of all the Scripture verses that are related to the theme you have chosen. Remember to consider synonyms and other similar words and concepts when using the concordance. Select from this list the verses that are most important to your theme (unless you are trying to discover *all* the Bible says about your theme).

STEP THREE   *Decide on the Questions You Will Ask*

How do you know what questions to ask? Write down those in which you are most interested. What are some things *you* would like to know about your theme? Make a list of questions, not more than five in number. Remember that sometimes you may need to ask only one question. Write your question(s) on the form or on a blank sheet of paper.

STEP FOUR *Ask Your Questions of Each Reference*

Read through your references, and ask your set of questions of each verse. Write down the answers you find in the appropriate places on your form or paper. Sometimes you will be able to answer all the questions for a given verse, but usually you will answer only part of them. Occasionally a verse may not answer any of your questions; in that case, leave that part blank on your form. If you are not finding any answers to your questions, start over and write a new set of questions.

STEP FIVE *Draw Some Conclusions from Your Study*

After you have finished checking the references and writing your answers, go back and summarize the answers to each of your questions. You might organize your study into an outline by grouping similar verses together and turning your questions into the major divisions of the outline. This will make it easy for you to share the insights you have discovered with others.

STEP SIX *Write Out a Personal Application*

To implement what you have discovered and make it real in your life, write out a personal application that is practical, possible, and measurable. Refer to the steps suggested in the Devotional Method (chap. 1) if you need help in developing an effective application.

HOW TO FILL IN THE THEMATIC STUDY FORM

Use either the Thematic Study Form you find at the end of this chapter or your own sheet of paper. If the form does not have enough room for all of your Scripture references, use additional sheets of paper.

Filling Out the Form

Fill in the blanks according to the following procedure:

1. *Theme:* Select the theme you want to research, being sure it is not too broad and is not a major topic.
2. *List of references:* List as many Scripture references as you need for your study.
3. *Questions to be asked:* List the questions (not more than five) you will be asking of each Scripture reference.
4. *Answers to the questions:* Ask the questions of each reference and write the answers in the appropriate space under each reference (Question A in all the A slots, Question B in the B slots, and so on throughout). Use extra sheets of paper if there is not enough room on the form.
5. *Conclusions:* Write out your conclusions and summaries of the verses studied.
6. *Application:* Write out a personal, practical, possible, and measurable application.

Sample Filled-out Form

See the example "Jesus' Definition of a Disciple" at the end of this chapter .

Assignment

Begin your thematic Bible studies with themes that are simple and have only a few Scripture references. As you become proficient in this method of Bible study, you can make your themes more complex and use more biblical passages. Here are some ideas to get you started, including sample questions you may ask. (Don't feel restricted by these suggested questions; make up some of your own for these themes.)

1. *Theme to be studied:* Knowing God's will. (Look up the word *will* in a concordance, and find the references to *God's will, will of God, will of the Lord, the Lord's will,* and any other related words.) Suggested questions:
   a. What specific things are God's will?
   b. Why am I to do God's will? (such things as motives and results)
   c. How am I to do God's will? (such things as attitudes and actions)
2. *Theme to be studied:* Obedience. (Look up the words *obey, obedience, keep, commandments, do,* and many others like them.) Suggested questions:
   a. Why is obedience important?
   b. What are the results of obedience?
   c. What are the results of disobedience?
   d. How am I to obey God?
3. *Theme to be studied:* Praising the Lord in the Psalms. (Note how this theme has been shortened to just the book of Psalms. Look up words such as *praise, adoration, thanksgiving,* and *joy.*) Suggested questions:
   a. Why should I praise the Lord?
   b. How can I praise the Lord?
   c. When should I praise the Lord?
   d. What are some results of praising the Lord?
4. *Theme to be studied:* The prayers of Jesus. (Note how this theme also has been shortened to one aspect of prayer. Look up this theme in a topical Bible and the words *pray* and *prayer* in a concordance, choosing only those found

in the Gospels in which Jesus is praying.) Here are some suggested questions, but you should be able to write many others of your own choosing:

a. How often should I pray?
b. When did Jesus pray?
c. Why should I pray as Jesus did?
d. What did Jesus pray for?
e. To whom should I pray?

FOR FURTHER READING

NIV Thematic Study Bible, edited by Alister McGrath (Hodder & Stoughton)
Zondervan Dictionary of Bible Themes, edited by Martin Manser (Zondervan)

THEMATIC STUDY FORM

1. THEME Jesus' Definition of a Disciple

2. LIST OF REFERENCES

> Matthew 10:24–25
> Luke 14:26–28
> Luke 14:33
> John 8:31–32
> John 13:34–35
> John 15:8

3. QUESTIONS TO BE ASKED

A. What are the characteristics of a disciple?

B. What are the results of being a disciple?

C.

D.

E.

4. ANSWERS TO QUESTIONS

Scripture Reference: Matthew 10:24–25

A. A disciple will be like Christ (his Master).

B. He should expect to be treated as Christ was by the world.

C.

D.

E.

THEMATIC STUDY FORM

Scripture Reference: Luke 14:26–28

    A. A disciple gives supreme love to Christ and bears his cross and follows Christ.

    B. (No answer given.)

    C.

    D.

    E.

Scripture Reference: Luke 14:33

    A. A disciple gives all to follow Christ.

    B. (No answer given.)

    C.

    D.

    E.

Scripture Reference: John 8:31–32

    A. A disciple continually abides in Christ's Word.

    B. He knows the truth and is set free.

    C.

    D.

    E.

THEMATIC STUDY FORM

Scripture Reference: John 13:34–35

    A. A disciple has love for others.

    B. Others will know that he belongs to Christ.

    C.

    D.

    E.

Scripture Reference: John 15:8

    A. A disciple bears fruit.

    B. His bearing fruit brings glory to God.

    C.

    D.

    E.

Scripture Reference:

    A.

    B.

    C.

    D.

    E.

THEMATIC STUDY FORM

5. CONCLUSIONS

Characteristics I discovered:

A disciple . . .

- is like Christ
- gives supreme love to Christ
- bears his cross and follows Christ
- gives up all to follow Christ
- continually abides in Christ's Word
- loves others
- bears fruit

Results I discovered:

- He should expect persecution.
- He knows the truth and is set free.
- He brings glory to God.
- Others notice he belongs to Christ.

6. APPLICATION

1. Based on John 8:31–32
   I will establish a regular, daily quiet time in the Word, starting tomorrow morning.
2. Based on John 13:34–35
   I will demonstrate love for the person in my Sunday school class who irritates me, and do so by asking his family to come to dinner this next week.

THEMATIC STUDY FORM

1. THEME

2. LIST OF REFERENCES

3. QUESTIONS TO BE ASKED

    A.

    B.

    C.

    D.

    E.

4. ANSWERS TO QUESTIONS

Scripture Reference:

    A.

    B.

    C.

    D.

    E.

THEMATIC STUDY FORM

Scripture Reference:

    A.

    B.

    C.

    D.

    E.

Scripture Reference:

    A.

    B.

    C.

    D.

    E.

Scripture Reference:

    A.

    B.

    C.

    D.

    E.

THEMATIC STUDY FORM

Scripture Reference:

    A.

    B.

    C.

    D.

    E.

Scripture Reference:

    A.

    B.

    C.

    D.

    E.

Scripture Reference:

    A.

    B.

    C.

    D.

    E.

THEMATIC STUDY FORM

5. CONCLUSIONS

6. APPLICATION

THE BIOGRAPHICAL METHOD OF BIBLE STUDY

5

How to Find Out What Made Bible People Tick

The Bible is composed of numerous stories of men and women and their relationships with the loving God who created them. To study the lives of these individuals is meaningful and uplifting. We can learn both what to do and what to be by looking at the positive attributes of hundreds of people who fill the pages of Scripture. We can also gain vast knowledge and wisdom by observing and avoiding the tremendous failures and negative aspects in the lives of people mentioned in God's Word.

DEFINITION

With the Biographical Method of Bible Study you select a biblical person and research the Scriptures to study their life and character. You try to become thoroughly acquainted with that person's inner life and find out what made it a spiritual success or failure. Ask God to help you think and feel with them so that your study becomes a life-changing experience.

The application of this study comes when you examine your own life in light of the study and ask God to help you make positive character changes in your weak areas. This will result in Christian growth and maturity.

THE IMPORTANCE OF BIBLE PEOPLE

People are important to God. We are made in his image and likeness, and the Bible is a record of his dealings with men and women. It is also a revelation of God himself, both *to* people and *through* people. To understand the Bible fully, you must get to know the prominent people of the Scriptures.

Much of the Old Testament is in narrative form, describing the lives of many people. The book of Genesis, for example, revolves around six great names: Adam, Noah, Abraham, Isaac, Jacob, Joseph. The apostle Paul said that God gave us the stories in the Old Testament to be examples to us, from which we should learn valuable lessons on living for him in this world. Paul wrote, "For everything that was written in the past was written to teach us, so that through the endurance taught in the Scriptures and the encouragement they provide we might have hope" (Rom. 15:4). He also said, "These things happened to [the people of the Old Testament] as examples and were written down as warnings for us, on whom the culmination of the ages has come" (1 Cor. 10:11).

The New Testament is a book of instructions; the Old Testament is a book of illustrations, though both Testaments contain instructions and illustrations. New Testament truths are illustrated in the Old Testament. One of the best ways to study the Old Testament is to study its people. This makes the older Scriptures really come alive.

The Bible mentions in greater or lesser detail more than 3,000 people. When you have learned this method of study, you will have opened the door to a lifetime of exciting, fulfilling Bible study. Biographical studies are enjoyable and are also one of the easiest methods from which to find personal applications.

TOOLS YOU WILL NEED

- Study Bible
- Exhaustive concordance
- Topical Bible
- Bible dictionary or encyclopedia

SOME TIPS FOR A GOOD BIOGRAPHICAL STUDY

To do a meaningful biographical study, keep the following pointers in mind.

1. Start with a person on whom you can do a simple study. Begin with one about whom there is a small number of references. Some biblical people can be studied in a few hours; others take weeks to study, and some major persons can take a lifetime. Do not start doing this study on a person such as Jesus, Moses, or Abraham. Begin with some minor but important people such as Andrew, Barnabas, or Mary of Bethany.

2. The secret of a good biographical study is to live with that person during the study. Walk in their sandals. Try to get inside their mind and see how they think, feel, and respond to circumstances. Attempt to see things from their point of view, hear with their ears, mingle with their friends, and fight with their enemies. *Become* that person while you are studying them. This is only possible if you spend much time with that person, reading and rereading all the Bible references about them.

A friend of mine, Wayne Watts, has spent a lifetime studying Abraham. He has studied this biblical person so long that he has taken on many characteristics of Abraham. He is a great man of faith, as Abraham was.

3. Be careful not to confuse different people who have the same name when you look up the references about them. You will have to

RICK WARREN'S BIBLE STUDY METHODS

STEP ONE — *Select the Bible Person You Want to Study*

STEP TWO — *Make a List of All the References about That Person*

STEP THREE — *Write Down First Impressions (First Reading)*

STEP FOUR — *Make a Chronological Outline (Second Reading)*

STEP FIVE — *Get Some Insights into the Person (Third Reading)*

STEP SIX — *Identify Some Character Qualities (Fourth Reading)*

STEP SEVEN — *Show How Other Bible Truths Are Illustrated in the Person's Life*

STEP EIGHT — *Summarize the Main Lesson(s)*

STEP NINE — *Write Out a Personal Application*

STEP TEN — *Make Your Study Transferable*

be sure that the verse is speaking about the person you have chosen to study. You would not want to confuse John the Baptist with John the Apostle or John Mark. For example, the Bible shows us that the following names were popular and refer to different people:

- Zechariah—30 different men
- Nathan—20 men
- Jonathan—15 men

- Judas—8 men
- Mary—7 women
- James—5 men
- John—5 men

The context of the verses will usually tell you which person is in view.

4. Be careful to find the various names that may apply to just one person. Since the Bible came out of a Hebrew-Aramaic-Greek context, some people's names changed in the different languages, in both the Old Testament and the New. The apostle Peter, for example, is known as Peter, Simon, Simeon, and Cephas. Daniel's three friends, Hananiah, Mishael, and Azariah, are better known as Shadrach, Meshach, and Abednego. Sometimes a name change came because of a character change, which was the case with Jacob becoming Israel. So be careful to find all the names used for the same person in your Bible study.

5. Stay away from books written about biblical people until after you have exhausted every Bible reference about that person and have drawn every possible insight out of those texts. Don't let a Bible commentary rob you of the task of personal discovery or prejudice your views of a person. Do your own work first, then check other sources.

SIMPLE STEPS ON DOING A BIOGRAPHICAL STUDY

The Biographical Study Form has 10 sections, which are the 10 steps for doing this study.

STEP ONE   *Select the Bible Person You Want to Study*

You might start out by selecting someone who has either a weakness that you have or a strength that you would like to develop. Choose a person whose life will give you some valuable insights into how you can conform more to God's standard for living and become more like Jesus Christ.

STEP TWO   *Make a List of All the References about That Person*

Using your reference tools, find all the Scripture passages you can about that person and things related to their life. This might include such things as their birth, major events of their life, their accomplishments, what others said about them, and their death. You will not be able to get all the necessary "vital statistics" about every person you study, but find out as much about them as you can.

Also look up any references that deal with the historical background of her life. If you were studying Esther, you would need to study the background of her day: the Persian Empire. If you were studying the apostle Paul, you would have to study his missionary journeys.

STEP THREE   *Write Down First Impressions (First Reading)*

Read through the Scripture references you have listed and make some notes. Write out the first impression you have of this person. Then write down some basic observations and important information you discover about him or her. Finally, list any problems, questions, or difficulties you wonder about as you read these references.

STEP FOUR   *Make a Chronological Outline (Second Reading)*

For a major biblical person, read all the references again and make a chronological outline of the person's life. This will help you gain a good perspective on their life, and you will see how different events relate to one another. Later, when you study the events associated with their life, you will know in what part of their life they occurred.

For minor biblical people or those about whose lives few details are given, read the references and make an outline on the basis of the information you have.

Try to read all the references in one sitting and in a modern translation. This will help you feel the flow of the person's life. As you read, look for any natural, major divisions in their life. Then look for and write down any progressions and changes of attitude in that person's life as times goes by. For example, a well-known division of Moses' life is

- Forty years in Pharaoh's court — learning to be a somebody
- Forty years in the Midian desert — learning to be a nobody
- Forty years in the Sinai desert — learning that God is Somebody

This process is a real key to studying the characters of the people involved. See how God slowly molded and changed the people or how Satan brought them down.

STEP FIVE   *Get Some Insights into the Person (Third Reading)*

Go back over the references again, and look for possible answers to the questions suggested in appendix B. By answering some of these questions, you should get some helpful insights into the character of the person you are studying.

STEP SIX   *Identify Some Character Qualities (Fourth Reading)*

As you review the references once again, use the suggested list of positive and negative characteristics in appendix C as a checklist. Write on your form or paper each quality, good or bad, that shows up in the person's life. Give a verse reference that shows each characteristic you have observed.

STEP SEVEN   *Show How Other Bible Truths Are Illustrated in the Person's Life*

Examine the person's life to see how it illustrates other truths taught in the Bible. For example, does their life show the principle of "you will reap what you sow"? Look in that life for illustrations of some of the Proverbs or of principles taught in the Psalms. For instance, you might ask, "Does his life illustrate the promise, 'Take delight in the Lord, and he will give you the desires of your heart'" (Ps. 37:4)? Find cross-references that illustrate what the Bible says about some of the characteristics you found in this person's life.

STEP EIGHT   *Summarize the Main Lesson(s)*

In a few sentences write out what you think is the main lesson that is taught or illustrated by this person's life. Is there any one word that could describe that life? What was their outstanding characteristic?

STEP NINE   *Write Out a Personal Application*

Refer to the Devotional Method of study (chap. 1) for the specifics of writing an application. In addition to the principles suggested there, you might ask yourself these questions:

- Did I see anything of myself in this person's life?
- Did he/she show some of my weaknesses?
- Did he/she reveal to me some of my strengths?
- What impressed me most about this person's life?
- Where do I fall short in this area?
- What do I intend to do about it?

STEP TEN   *Make Your Study Transferable*

Condense what you have learned into a simple outline that will help you remember it and enable you to share your conclusions with others. Make it "pass-on-able." Ask yourself, "What can this person's life mean to others? What can I share that I have learned that would help someone else?"

Divide the information into natural sequences of time and/or events and lessons learned. Use the progressions that you have found and recorded. Then think of some easily remembered ways to title each section. Keep these titles true to the major content of each section, making use of rhymes, alliterations, and other memory devices. Use your imagination in this last step!

An illustration of a transferable outline of the life of Barnabas might look like this:

- He was an *investor* of money in the lives of church members (Acts 4:36 – 37).
- He was the *introducer* of Saul (later Paul) to the apostles (Acts 9:26 – 28).
- He was the *inspector* of the new church at Antioch (Acts 11:22 – 24).
- He was an *instructor* of new Christians, including Paul and Mark (Acts 11:22 – 26; 15:39).
- He was the *initiator* on the first missionary journey, which he began as the team leader but ended as a team member (Acts 13 – 14).
- He was an *interpreter* of the doctrine of salvation and God's plan for the Gentiles (Acts 13 – 14).
- He was *insistent* in giving Mark another chance to be trained in the gospel ministry (Acts 15:36 – 39).

CONCLUSION

In the 10-step procedure just given, it is suggested that you read all your references through four times. Actually, this is *a minimum* number. The more times you review the passages about the person you are studying, the more you are going to observe. (See the observation sections in chapter 10 of this book.)

HOW TO FILL IN THE BIOGRAPHICAL STUDY FORM

At the end of this chapter is a Biographical Study Form that you can reproduce or use as a guide for writing on your own sheets of paper. The form lists the 10 steps already discussed for doing this study.

Filling Out the Form

Fill in the blanks of each of the 10 parts as described in the section above. If you need more room, use the back of the form or allow more room on your own paper.

Sample Filled-out Form

See the example on the life of Stephen at the end of this chapter.

Assignment

Appendix D provides lists of the major and minor men and prominent women of the Bible. Select from those lists any people who particularly interest you. If you are just beginning this method of study, you might want to do the following people first:

- Mary of Bethany
- Andrew
- Caleb
- Ruth
- Daniel

For Further Reading

Many books have been written on the men and women of the Bible. The ones listed here are some of the better ones. Remember, however, not to read the books before doing your study; do your study first, then check to see what others have discovered about that person.

All of the Women of the Bible by Edith Deen (HarperSanFrancisco)

All the Men of the Bible by Herbert Lockyer (Zondervan)

All the Women of the Bible by Herbert Lockyer (Zondervan)

The Complete Book of Who's Who in the Bible by Philip Comfort and Walter Elwell (Tyndale)

Her Name Is Woman, books I and 2, by Gien Karssen (NavPress)

Lost Women of the Bible by Carolyn Custis James (Zondervan)

Making of a Man of God (on David) by Alan Redpath (Revell)

Men of the Bible by Ann Spangler and Robert Wolgemuth (Zondervan)

New International Encyclopedia of Bible Characters, edited by Paul Gardner (Zondervan)

The Oxford Guide to People and Places of the Bible, edited by Bruce Metzger and Michael Coogan (Oxford University Press)

Robust in Faith by J. Oswald Sanders (Moody Press)

Women of the Bible by Ann Spangler and Jean Syswerda (Zondervan)

BIOGRAPHICAL STUDY FORM

1. NAME Stephen

2. SCRIPTURE REFERENCES

Acts 6:3–8:2
Acts 11:19
Acts 22:20

3. FIRST IMPRESSIONS AND OBSERVATIONS

Stephen was an early Christian who had a tremendous testimony in the church, was a powerful preacher and witness, and was willing to die for his faith.

4. OUTLINE OF HIS OR HER LIFE

A. Chosen by the early church as a leader—
   1. to help resolve a conflict (Acts 6:5)
   2. on the basis of certain godly characteristics (Acts 6:3, 5, 8)
B. He had a wide ministry—
   1. waited on tables (Acts 6:2, 5)
   2. performed miracles (Acts 6:8)
   3. preached and taught powerfully (Acts 6:10)
C. He was persecuted—
   1. opposed by Jews from "overseas" (Acts 6:9)
   2. falsely accused (Acts 6:11)
   3. arrested and brought before the Sanhedrin (Acts 6:12–14)
      a. had false witnesses testify against him
      b. defended himself with a masterful review of O.T. Scripture (Acts 7:2–53)
      c. testified to Jesus (Acts 7:55–56)
      d. stoned by an angry mob (Acts 7:57–60)
D. He had a ministry after his death—persecution caused the church to spread (Acts 8:2–4; 11:19)

BIOGRAPHICAL STUDY FORM

5. GENERAL INSIGHTS (Answers to questions)

A. Why was he chosen to be a leader?
  - He was full of the Holy Spirit and wisdom (Acts 6:3).
  - He was full of faith and the Spirit (Acts 6:5).
  - He was full of God's grace and power (Acts 6:8).
  - He knew the Scriptures (Acts 7:2–53).

B. What was his response to false accusations? He "kept his cool," remained silent, and only answered when he was directed to speak by the high priest.

C. Are there any parallels with Jesus? Yes, he was falsely accused, demonstrated love and concern for his accusers, and died an "undeserved" death.

D. What was his attitude toward his executioners? He was forgiving, even to the point of praying that God would forgive them for their sin of murder.

E. What were the long-term results of his life, ministry, and death?
  - They forwarded the plan of God.
  - His death caused the disciples to scatter and take the gospel to other parts of Judea, Samaria, and regions beyond Palestine in fulfillment of Acts 1:8.
  - His death also helped bring Paul to the Lord.

BIOGRAPHICAL STUDY FORM

6. CHARACTER QUALITIES IDENTIFIED The Book of Acts

- Spirit-filled (6:3, 5, 10)
- Wise (6:3, 10)
- Faithful (6:5)
- Available to God (6:8)
- Persistent (6:10)
- Holy (6:15)
- Knowledgeable (chap. 7)
- Bold (7:51–53)
- Brave (7:51–53)
- Forgiving (7:60)
- Respected by others (8:2)
- A witness to Jesus (22:20)

7. BIBLE TRUTHS ILLUSTRATED IN HIS OR HER LIFE

- The presence and comfort of the Holy Spirit in the trials of life (Acts 7:54–55; Hebrews 13:5–6).
- False accusations and persecution will come into our lives (Acts 6:11ff.).
- God's grace is sufficient when we walk with him (Acts 6:10; 1 Cor. 1:27–31; 2 Cor. 12:9).

8. SUMMARY OF LESSONS LEARNED FROM HIS OR HER LIFE

The outstanding characteristic of Stephen was his commitment to the Lord and his willingness to do anything for him, including giving up his life.

This commitment is seen in the fact that he was a man who walked with God (he was "full of the Spirit and wisdom ... faith ... God's grace and power"). He had a great testimony before others in the church. He witnessed to people both in life and in death.

He was, furthermore, a man of the Word. He really knew his Bible—the Old Testament. He must have spent hours studying the scrolls and the parchments.

BIOGRAPHICAL STUDY FORM

9. PERSONAL APPLICATION

I need to become a person like Stephen—a person of the Word who knows Jesus Christ intimately and who is able to answer others with Scripture when they ask questions. As a result of this study, I will commit myself to having a daily quiet time for at least 15 minutes to get to know Christ better. I will also commit myself to memorizing two Scripture verses each week so that I can answer people who ask me questions.

10. TRANSFERABLE CONCEPTS   (Ways I can share this with others)

The concepts in this study that are transferable:
A. The necessity of a personal walk with Jesus Christ. The only way we can become men and women of faith and wisdom like Stephen is to have a daily quiet time with the Lord. Stephen had a dynamic walk with Jesus Christ.
B. The necessity of being in the Word of God on a regular basis—Bible study and Scripture memory. If I am to know my Bible as Stephen did, I need to spend quality time in it and be able to teach others how to do so as well. This book is one means to help me do so. I need to share these methods with others.
C. The necessity of courage in times of adversity and persecution. I need to pray that God will give me boldness with others.

11. SOMEONE WITH WHOM I INTEND TO SHARE THIS STUDY

Pat Conner and Tommy Pauter (by email)

RICK WARREN'S BIBLE STUDY METHODS

BIOGRAPHICAL STUDY FORM

1. NAME

2. SCRIPTURE REFERENCES

3. FIRST IMPRESSIONS AND OBSERVATIONS

4. OUTLINE OF HIS OR HER LIFE

---------- BIOGRAPHICAL STUDY FORM ----------

5. GENERAL INSIGHTS (Answers to questions)

BIOGRAPHICAL STUDY FORM

6. CHARACTER QUALITIES IDENTIFIED

7. BIBLE TRUTHS ILLUSTRATED IN HIS OR HER LIFE

8. SUMMARY OF LESSONS LEARNED FROM HIS OR HER LIFE

BIOGRAPHICAL STUDY FORM

9. PERSONAL APPLICATION

10. TRANSFERABLE CONCEPTS (Ways I can share this with others)

11. SOMEONE WITH WHOM I INTEND TO SHARE THIS STUDY

6

THE TOPICAL METHOD OF BIBLE STUDY

How to Trace a Topic through Scripture

One of the most exciting ways to study the Bible is by examining topics. The Topical Method is similar to the Thematic Method (see chap. 4), but there are some important differences. One is that the Topical Method usually takes longer than the Thematic Method because we study more verses. A topic usually has many minor themes running through it, and in a topical study we consider *all* of the related themes. Another difference is that with the Topical Method we do not decide ahead of time what questions we want to ask. Instead, we examine each verse without predetermined guidelines and record *all* of the insights we discover. We do not limit our study to just finding the answers to four or five questions as in the Thematic Method.

DEFINITION

The Topical Method of Bible Study involves selecting a biblical subject and tracing it through a single book, from either the Old or New Testament, or through the entire Bible in order to discover what God says about the topic. It uses extensive cross-referencing, and the questions you ask of a given text are limitless. Some good examples of topical studies based on the King James Version may be found in the back of the *Thompson Chain Reference Bible* and in *Dickson's New Analytical Study Bible* (World Publishers). For studies built on a contemporary Bible version, see the *Zondervan Dictionary of Bible Themes* (edited by Martin Manser [Zondervan]) and the *NIV Thematic Study Bible* (edited by Alister McGrath [Hodder & Stoughton]). Every book contains a number of topics that the writer has carefully woven together. The Topical Method can be used to study a doctrine, an idea, a phrase, or basically any subject that is mentioned in the Bible.

THE IMPORTANCE OF THE TOPICAL STUDY

The Topical Method is important for the following reasons:

1. It enables us to study the Word of God systematically, logically, and in an orderly manner.
2. It gives us a proper perspective and balance regarding biblical truth. We get to see the whole of a biblical teaching.
3. It allows us to study subjects that are of particular interest to us.
4. It enables us to study the great doctrines of the Bible.
5. It lends itself to good and lively discussions. The results of a topical study are always easy to share with others.
6. It allows us variety in our lifetime commitment to personal Bible study. The number of topics in the Bible that we can study is almost limitless.

TOOLS YOU WILL NEED

The reference tools you will need for this method of study are the standard ones. Remember that no topical Bible has every verse on

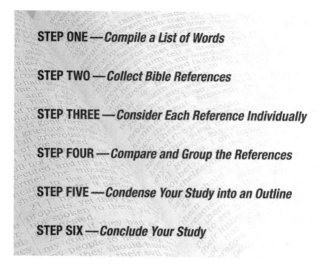

STEP ONE —*Compile a List of Words*

STEP TWO —*Collect Bible References*

STEP THREE —*Consider Each Reference Individually*

STEP FOUR —*Compare and Group the References*

STEP FIVE —*Condense Your Study into an Outline*

STEP SIX —*Conclude Your Study*

any given topic. If you want to do a thorough study on a selected topic, you will have to use an exhaustive concordance. The needed tools are

- A study Bible
- An exhaustive concordance
- A topical Bible

SUGGESTIONS FOR A GOOD TOPICAL STUDY

Dr. R. A. Torrey, a great Bible scholar and teacher, gives three suggestions that are helpful in studying the Bible topically *(How to Study the Bible,* Whitaker House). These are

1. *Be systematic.* Don't try to study the Bible in a haphazard manner that is basically undisciplined. Make a list of all the things related to your topic, and make it as comprehensive and complete as possible. Then take up these items one at a time, studying them in a systematic and logical order.

2. *Be thorough.* As far as possible, find and study *every* verse that relates to the topic. The only way to know everything God has said on a topic is to go through the entire Bible and find all the passages on that topic. Use your concordance to do this.

3. *Be exact.* Try to get the exact meaning of every verse you study. Be sure to examine the context of each verse to avoid misinterpretation. The biggest mistake you must avoid is taking a verse out of its context.

SIMPLE STEPS ON DOING A TOPICAL STUDY

Essentially, a topical study is built around six steps, each of which can be summarized with one word:

1. *Compile* a list of all the words related to the topic.
2. *Collect* all the references.
3. *Consider* each verse individually.
4. *Compare* all the references with one another.
5. *Condense* your finding into an outline.
6. *Conclude* by summarizing and applying the topic.

Before starting on the six steps, choose a topic that interests you. It may be specifically mentioned or merely implied in the text, but it should be important, both in content and in personal interest. When you use this method of study for the first time, pick a topic that is not too vast or time-consuming. You might restrict your topic to references found in a testament or a single book of the Bible.

STEP ONE   *Compile a List of Words*

Make a list of all the related words (synonyms and antonyms), phrases, events, and anything else that could have something to do with your topic. If you are studying *suffering*, for example, you will want to list words such as *affliction, anger, chastisement, grief, health, pain, sor-*

row, trials, and *tribulation.* If you see that your topic has become too broad, narrow it down to a manageable size.

STEP TWO   *Collect Bible References*

Take your reference tools and begin to gather all the verses you can find on the topic. Look up in your concordance each related word listed in Step One. Make a list of all verses that relate in any way to the topic. Also, you will want to use your topical Bible to find verses for study.

STEP THREE   *Consider Each Reference Individually*

Using the Comparison Chart at the end of this chapter, look up, read, and study each individual reference and write down your observations and insights on it. (You will use the Comparison Chart for both Step Three and Step Four.) Be sure to check the context (surrounding verses) carefully when studying a verse, to make sure you are interpreting it correctly.

Ask as many questions as you can about each verse you study. Remember to use the great what, why, when, where, who, and how questions. Don't forget to define all key words you come across.

STEP FOUR   *Compare and Group the References*

After you have carefully studied all your verses individually, you will begin to notice that some of the references naturally complement each other and deal with the same areas of the topic under study. Categorize these references on a piece of scratch paper.

STEP FIVE   *Condense Your Study into an Outline*

Using the categories from Step Four, logically arranged as your main divisions, outline your study. Do this by grouping related or similar references together into natural divisions. Then organize these divisions into a logical pattern. In helping you organize your study, this step will also enable you to share it with others.

STEP SIX   *Conclude Your Study*

In your two-part conclusion, summarize your findings in a brief paragraph and then write out a practical application drawn from this summary. Remember to be personal and practical, writing a possible and measurable application.

HOW TO FILL IN THE TOPICAL STUDY FORM

At the end of this chapter is a Topical Study Form that you can reproduce or print out.

Filling Out the Form

Follow the steps just given, adding extra forms for Step Three and Step Four as needed and using additional sheets of paper if you need space for Step Five and Step Six in a longer study. Follow this procedure:

- *Topic:* Select the topic and write in the first blank the exact name of what you plan to study.
- *List of words:* Write out any words related to the topic that you will be looking up in a concordance and topical Bible.
- *Bible references:* Make a list of all the Scripture references you have found that deal with your topic.
- *Comparison Chart* (for Steps Three and Four): Fill in the chart this way:
    1. References — write out the verse(s) from the Bible version of your choice or just list each reference.

    2. Cross-references—find some other verses in the Bible that complement or shed light on the verse you are studying.

    3. Observation and insights—record the insights you find.

- *Comparisons and grouping:* After you have filled out your chart on each verse, compare the verses with one another. Begin grouping similar verses together on a sheet of scratch paper.
- *Condensed outline:* Using the categories you developed in Step Four, make an outline of your study. There is no one right way to outline your study, so do it the way that is easiest for you.
- *Conclusion:* Write out a summary of your conclusions in this space. Then write out a way you can apply what you've learned to your life.

Sample Filled-out Form

See the example "The Faithful Man" at the end of this chapter.

Assignment

A topical study is one of the most interesting ways you can approach the Bible, and the number of topics to choose from is limitless. Here are some suggestions of major categories in the Bible that could be studied topically:

1. Doctrines	7. Attitudes
2. Miracles	8. Animals
3. Prayers	9. The Family
4. Problems	10. Great Questions
5. Promises	11. Duties to God
6. Prophecies	12. Disciple-making

For Further Reading

Numerous valuable books are available on topics found in the Bible. Some of the most useful in this area are written by Dr. Herbert Lockyer and published by Zondervan.

All the Doctrines of the Bible
All the Prayers of the Bible
All the Miracles of the Bible
All the Prophecies of the Bible
All the Promises of the Bible

See also the books and Bibles mentioned earlier in the chapter.

RICK WARREN'S BIBLE STUDY METHODS

——— TOPICAL STUDY FORM ———

TOPIC The Faithful Man (2 Timothy 2:2)

1. COMPILE A LIST OF WORDS

Faithful

2. COLLECT BIBLE REFERENCES

1 Samuel 2:35
1 Samuel 22:14
Nehemiah 7:2
Nehemiah 13:13
Isaiah 8:2
Daniel 6:4
Psalm 12:1
Proverbs 20:6
Proverbs 28:20
Matthew 24:45
Luke 16:10–13
Luke 19:17
1 Corinthians 1:9
1 Corinthians 4:1–2, 16–17
1 Corinthians 10:13
Ephesians 6:21
Colossians 1:7
Colossians 4:7, 9
1 Timothy 1:12
2 Timothy 2:2
1 Peter 5:12
1 John 1:9

TOPICAL STUDY FORM

COMPARISON CHART

3. CONSIDER EACH REFERENCE INDIVIDUALLY
4. COMPARE AND GROUP THE REFERENCES

Reference	Cross-References	Observations and Insights
Numbers 12:7		• Moses was called faithful by God.
1 Samuel 2:35		• It was prophesied that Samuel would be a faithful man. • A faithful man is obedient to God's will.
1 Samuel 22:14		• David was called a faithful man by Ahimelech.
Nehemiah 7:2	Matthew 24:45	• Hanani was called a faithful man by Nehemiah. • A faithful man is given leadership roles.
Nehemiah 9:7–8		• Abraham was considered faithful by the Lord.
Nehemiah 13:13		• Nehemiah considered his treasurers faithful, so he gave them responsibility.
Isaiah 8:2		• Uriah and Zechariah were faithful witnesses in the sight of the Lord.
Daniel 6:4	John 19:4	• The Persian princes could not accuse Daniel of any wrongdoing, because he was a faithful man. • A faithful man lives a blameless testimony before the world.
Psalm 12:1	Proverbs 20:6 Philippians 2:19–20	• Faithful people are few in number and hard to find.

RICK WARREN'S BIBLE STUDY METHODS

TOPICAL STUDY FORM
COMPARISON CHART

Reference	Cross-References	Observations and Insights
Proverbs 20:6	Philippians 2:19–22	• There are not many faithful people in the world. • A faithful man cares about the interests of others, while an unfaithful man is always bragging about himself and serving himself.
Proverbs 28:20		• A faithful man abounds with blessing. • A faithful man has his values right, in contrast with someone who is eager to get rich.
Matthew 24:45	Nehemiah 7:2	• A faithful man is given leadership roles.
Matthew 25:21, 23	Luke 19:17	• A faithful servant will be rewarded with greater responsibilities in heaven and will experience the Lord's joy over his faithfulness.
Luke 16:10–13		• This passage shows four ways to test a person's faithfulness: (1) Test him in small things before giving him big things. (2) Test him in nonspiritual matters before giving him spiritual truth. (3) Test him in how he values what isn't his. (4) Test his commitment to God.
Luke 19:17	Matthew 25:21, 23	• A faithful servant is rewarded with greater responsibility.
1 Corinthians 1:9	1 Corinthians 10:13 1 John 1:9	• God is faithful.

TOPICAL STUDY FORM
COMPARISON CHART

Reference	Cross-References	Observations and Insights
1 Corinthians 4:1 – 2		• A faithful man demonstrates wise stewardship.
1 Corinthians 4:16 – 17	Ephesians 6:21 Colossians 1:7 Colossians 4:7, 9	• Timothy was called a faithful man by Paul. A faithful man's discipler shows confidence in him by sending him in his place.
1 Corinthians 10:13	1 Corinthians 1:9 1 John 1:9	• God is faithful.
Ephesians 6:21	Colossians 4:7	• Tychicus was called a faithful minister by Paul.
Colossians 1:7		• Epaphras was a faithful minister of Jesus Christ.
Colossians 4:7	Ephesians 6:21	• Tychicus was sent by Paul to the Colossians because he was a reliable, faithful man.
Colossians 4:9		• Onesimus was considered faithful by Paul.
1 Timothy 1:12		• God considered Paul faithful. • A faithful man will be given a ministry.
2 Timothy 2:2		• A faithful man is entrusted with spiritual truth. • A faithful man passes on to others what he has learned.
1 Peter 5:12		• Silas was called faithful by Peter.

TOPICAL STUDY FORM

5. CONDENSED OUTLINE

I. Faithfulness Is a Godly Quality
   A. 1 Corinthians 1:9
   B. 1 Corinthians 10:13
   C. 1 John 1:9
II. Faithful Men Are Hard to Find
   A. Psalm 12:1
   B. Proverbs 20:6
   C. Philippians 2:19 – 20
III. Biblical Examples of Faithful Men
   A. Old Testament Examples
      1. Abraham — Nehemiah 9:7 – 8
      2. Moses — Numbers 12:7
      3. Samuel — 1 Samuel 2:35
      4. David — 1 Samuel 22:14
      5. Hanani — Nehemiah 7:2
      6. Nehemiah's treasurers — Nehemiah 13:13
      7. Uriah and Zechariah — Isaiah 8:2
      8. Daniel — Daniel 6:4
   B. New Testament Examples
      1. Timothy — 1 Corinthians 4:17
      2. Tychicus — Ephesians 6:21
      3. Epaphras — Colossians 1:7
      4. Onesimus — Colossians 4:9
      5. Paul — 1 Timothy 1:12
      6. Silas — 1 Peter 5:12
   C. Insights
      1. Many men called faithful in the New Testament received training from Paul.
      2. Paul himself was a faithful man. He was an example to those he trained.
IV. Characteristics of a Faithful Man
   A. He cares for others' interests, not his own (Prov. 20:6; Phil. 2:19 – 22).
   B. He has his values right. He is not anxious to get rich (Prov. 28:20).
   C. He lives a blameless testimony before the world (Dan. 6:4).
   D. He is obedient to God's will (1 Sam. 2:35).
   E. He demonstrates wise stewardship (1 Cor. 4:1 – 2).
   F. He passes on to others what he has learned (2 Tim. 2:2).

TOPICAL STUDY FORM

V. Ways to Test a Man's Faithfulness (Luke 16:10–13)

  A. Test him in small responsibilities before giving him large ones (v. 10).

  B. Test him in nonspiritual matters before giving him spiritual truth (v. 11).

  C. Test him in how he values what isn't his, before giving him his own. Observe how he serves faithfully in someone else's ministry before sending him out on his own (v. 12).

  D. Test him in his commitment to God (v. 13).

VI.The Benefits of Being a Faithful Man

  A. He is given leadership roles (Neh. 7:2; Matt. 24:45).

  B. He will abound with blessing (Prov. 28:20).

  C. He will be rewarded with greater responsibilities in heaven and will experience the Lord's joy over his faithfulness (Matt. 25:21, 23; Luke 19:17).

  D. He is given a ministry (1 Tim. 1:12).

  E. He is entrusted with spiritual truth (2 Tim. 2:2).

  F. His discipler shows confidence in him by sending him in his place (1 Cor. 4:16–17; Phil. 2:19–24; Eph. 6:21).

──── TOPICAL STUDY FORM ────

6. CONCLUSION **(Summary and Application)**

As I did this study on the faithful man, God impressed on me the need to be more faithful in two specific areas. First, I need to be more faithful in my prayer life; I have to be more disciplined in setting aside a daily period for prayer. Second, I need to be more faithful in my finances. Luke 16:10 is a verse I needed. It teaches that if I am not faithful in handling my money, God will not trust me with true riches—spiritual blessings.

Projects

- I plan to memorize the passage on "tests of a man's faithfulness" by next week: Luke 16:10–13.
- I will set up a family budget with my wife this weekend. We will start keeping better records of how we spend our money and will ask God to guide us in our spending, saving, and giving.
- I will begin spending 20 minutes each morning before breakfast to review my prayer list and pray.

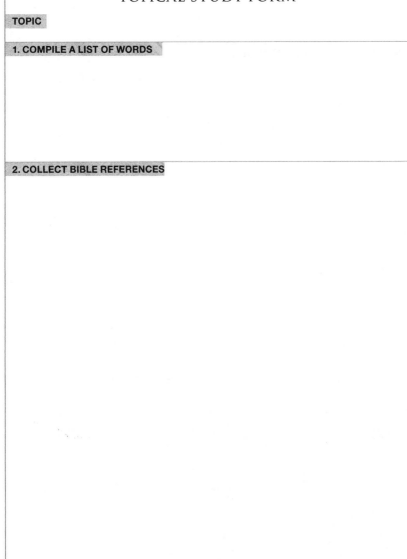

TOPICAL STUDY FORM

TOPIC

1. COMPILE A LIST OF WORDS

2. COLLECT BIBLE REFERENCES

TOPICAL STUDY FORM
COMPARISON CHART

3. CONSIDER EACH REFERENCE INDIVIDUALLY
4. COMPARE AND GROUP THE REFERENCES

Reference	Cross-References	Observations and Insights

—————— TOPICAL STUDY FORM ——————

5. CONDENSED OUTLINE

TOPICAL STUDY FORM

6. CONCLUSION (Summary and Application)

THE WORD STUDY METHOD OF BIBLE STUDY

7

How to Discover the Meanings of Bible Words

The Bible was originally written in Hebrew, Aramaic, and Greek. Even though the average Christian does not know these languages, we can still do word studies because of the availability of many excellent translations and reference tools. In the past, people who were interested in doing personal Bible study had to learn the original languages. Only those who had spent years learning Greek and Hebrew were able to enjoy the exciting insights that come from studying the original words of Scripture. Today, however, the riches to be found in word studies are within reach of every Christian who knows what tools are available.

DEFINITION

The Word Study Method of Bible Study takes a microscopic look at the origin, definition, occurrences, and uses of a particular word, especially as it relates to the context of a passage of Scripture. The purpose is to learn as precisely and comprehensively as possible what the biblical writer meant by the word he used.

WHY YOU SHOULD STUDY WORDS IN THE BIBLE

Irving Jensen has said, "Just as a great door swings on small hinges, so the important theological statements of the Bible often depend upon even the smallest words, such as prepositions and articles" (*Enjoy Your Bible*, World Wide Publications, p. 96). Most of the great doctrines of the Word of God revolve around a single word, such as *grace, atonement,* or *faith.* In order to understand the deepest meaning of Scripture, we must study the specific words that were used.

Correct interpretation of biblical truths depends on the correct understanding of the words used to convey these truths. David declared, "The words of the LORD are flawless, like silver purified in a crucible, like gold refined seven times" (Ps. 12:6). One of the writers

STEP ONE — *Choose Your Word*

STEP TWO — *Find Its English Definition*

STEP THREE — *Compare Translations*

STEP FOUR — *Write down the Definition of the Original Word*

STEP FIVE — *Check the Word's Occurrences in the Bible*

STEP SIX — *Find the Root Meaning and Origin of the Word*

STEP SEVEN — *Discover the Word's Usage in the Bible*

STEP EIGHT — *Write Out an Application*

of Proverbs stated similarly, "Every word of God is flawless; he is a shield to those who take refuge in him" (Prov. 30:5).

But these flawless words were written in a language other than ours, and their full meanings are not always transmitted completely through a translation. In fact, no translation is perfect, because no two languages correspond exactly. Word equivalents do not always exist between languages, so in studying the Bible we may have to search out the full meaning of a word that the translators were unable to squeeze into the chosen text.

Furthermore, when the original text of the Bible was translated into English, some 6,000 different words were used, whereas in the Hebrew, Aramaic, and Greek original, 11,280 words were used (Jensen, *Enjoy Your Bible*, p. 96). So how do you fit 11,000 words into 6,000? By translating several different original-language words into one English word. For example, in the New Testament the English word *servant* translates seven different Greek words, each of which had a slightly different shade of meaning for a servant. Our language, a later one, is unable to completely give the full meanings of the original biblical languages.

We must keep two things in mind when doing a word study. First, our word studies must be based on the original-language words, not on the English words. Second, we must always allow the context to indicate the ultimate meaning of the word being studied, no matter what the English equivalent might be.

TOOLS YOU WILL NEED

For this method of Bible study, you will need more reference tools than you have used with other methods. The necessary tools are

- A study Bible.
- Several recent translations. (These will enable you to see the words different translators chose from the original ones. Do *not* use paraphrases in this study.)

- An exhaustive concordance.
- A Bible dictionary and/or encyclopedia.
- A set of word studies (see the Introduction to this book).
- A good English dictionary.
- If you have had some Greek, *The Englishman's Greek Concordance of the New Testament* (Zondervan) will be useful.
- *The Word Study Concordance* and its companion volume, *The Word Study New Testament*, by Ralph Winter (William Carey Library).

THREE COMMON DIFFICULTIES IN DOING WORD STUDIES

As you begin this method of Bible study, you need to be aware of some difficulties you might run into.

1. *Sometimes several Greek words are translated by just one English word.* We have already noted that the English word *servant* has seven Greek equivalents, each with a different shade of meaning. Be sure to check your concordance carefully to see if this might be true of the word you are studying. Find out what each different original word meant.

2. *Sometimes one Greek or Hebrew word is translated several ways in English.* To overcome this difficulty you will have to do a careful study on all the different renderings of that original word. You can do this quite easily through the use of your exhaustive concordance. For example, the Greek word *koinonia* is translated five different ways in the King James Version: (1) "communication" — once; (2) "communion" — 4 times; (3) "contribution" — once; (4) "distribution" — once; and (5) "fellowship" — 12 times.

Follow this procedure in solving this difficulty:

- List the different ways the word is translated.
- List how many times it is translated each way.

- Give examples of each translation (if possible).
- Write down how the different meanings might be related.
- Determine if the writer of the book is using the word you are studying in a single sense or is giving it a multiple meaning.

3. *Sometimes an original word is translated by a whole phrase in English.* This difficulty will take a little more work to overcome because concordances do not list word translations by phrases. You will have to compare the recent versions of the Bible you are using to see how the various translators have rendered the word. For example, Paul declared to the Corinthians, "But we all, with open face beholding as in a glass the glory of the Lord, are changed into the same image from glory to glory, even as by the Spirit of the Lord" (2 Cor. 3:18 KJV). The phrase "beholding as in a glass" is just one word in the original Greek (*katoptrizomenoi*), and you will discover some interesting truths when you study the origin of that word.

SIMPLE STEPS ON DOING A WORD STUDY

The Word Study Form has eight sections, one for each of the steps in this study, and a space for listing the reference tools that you use in doing it.

STEP ONE *Choose Your Word*

In your previous personal Bible study, you may have wondered what certain words meant. Choose a word that you wondered about or are interested in, or choose one from the list in appendix E.

STEP TWO *Find Its English Definition*

Use your English dictionary and write out the definition of the English word. List with the definition any synonyms or antonyms of the word.

STEP THREE   *Compare Translations*

Read in different recent translations the passages where this word is used. Write down the different renderings of the word that you find. Take note of any renderings that are repeatedly and commonly used in these translations.

STEP FOUR   *Write Down the Definition of the Original Word*

Find out what the original word is in your exhaustive concordance or word study book and write down its definition. You may find it has a number of usages.

STEP FIVE   *Check the Word's Occurrences in the Bible*

Using your concordance again, find out how and where the word is used in the Bible. Ask these questions:

- How many times does the word occur in the Bible?
- In what books does it occur?
- What writers used the word?
- In what book does it occur most?
- Where does the word occur first in the Bible?
- Where does it occur first in the book I am studying?

STEP SIX   *Find the Root Meaning and Origin of the Word*

This step brings you into some research. You will want to read a fuller discussion of the meaning and origin of the word you are studying, using a Bible dictionary, a Bible encyclopedia, a word study set, or a theological word book.

STEP SEVEN	*Discover the Word's Usage in the Bible*

Here you will want to find out how the word is used in the Bible. The study of the root meaning (Step Six) told you what the word meant *originally* and where it came from, but some words change their meanings with the passage of time. Also, they might have different meanings in different situations and contexts. In the final analysis, the usage of a word is the most important factor in determining its true meaning. Fulfill this step in the following three ways:

1. *Find out how the word was used during the time the book of the Bible was written.* How was it used in other writings besides the Bible? To find out what the word meant and how it was used in the culture of the day, you will have to look at extrabiblical materials (for example, histories of the time); many times, however, the word study set you are using will have this information. Advanced students and people who know the original languages may find this information in theological dictionaries and Hebrew and Greek lexicons.

2. *Find out how the word is used in the Bible.* Using your exhaustive concordance, find out how the word is translated every time it appears in the Bible. Often the Scriptures define words through usage and illustrations; this is a way of finding out the scriptural definition. You may also ask some or all of the following questions:

- How does the writer use the word in other parts of the book?
- How does the writer use the word in other books he has written?
- How is the word used throughout the whole testament?
- Does the word have more than one usage? If so, what are its other uses?
- What is the most frequent use of the word?
- How is it used the first time in the Scriptures?

3. *Find out how the word is used in the context of the passage.* This is the ultimate test. The context will be your most reliable source for insights into what the writer really meant. Ask these questions:

- Does the context give any clues to the meaning of the word?
- Is the word compared or contrasted with another word in the context?
- Is there any illustration in the context that clarifies the meaning of the word?

STEP EIGHT   *Write Out an Application*

Be especially careful to keep your goal of "application, not interpretation only" in mind when you do a word study. Remember that you are doing *personal* Bible study, not just conducting an academic exercise. Discovering the full meaning of a biblical word is not an end in itself, because a word study without application has little spiritual value. In doing this study, constantly ask yourself, "How can understanding this word strengthen my spiritual life?" So write out an application, using the suggestions in chapter 1.

RESOURCE BOOKS USED

The last blank section on your study form has a place to list the reference tools you used in your word study. This is to help you remember the most useful resource books for use in the future.

HOW TO FILL IN THE WORD STUDY FORM

Use the Word Study Form at the end of this chapter or your own sheet of paper with the same divisions.

Filling Out the Form

Follow the steps outlined above and write in the discoveries you make. If you need more room, use the back of the form or sheet.

Sample Filled-out Form

See the example of the word *repent* in the sample filled-out form at the end of this chapter.

Assignment

You may want to start this Bible study method by studying words you have been wondering about. Or you may want to begin with some important doctrinal words. A suggested list of words is provided in appendix E.

For Further Reading

The Complete Word-Study Dictionary of the Old Testament by Eugene Carpenter (AMG)

Gems from the Original by Harold J. Berry (Back to the Bible)

The New International Dictionary of New Testament Theology: Abridged Edition, edited by Verlyn Verbrugge (Zondervan)

New Testament Words by William Barclay (Westminster John Knox)

A Theological Word Book of the Bible, edited by Alan Richardson (Macmillan)

A Theological Word Book of the Old Testament, edited by Laird Harris et al. (Moody Press)

Vincent's Word Studies in the New Testament by Marvin R. Vincent (Hendrickson)

WORD STUDY FORM

1. ENGLISH WORD   Repent (noun—Repentance)

2. ENGLISH DEFINITION

"To feel such remorse or regret for past conduct as to change one's mind regarding it."

3. COMPARISON OF TRANSLATIONS   Luke 13:3

"Repent"—NIV, NASB, KJV, *Amplified*, etc.
"Turn from your sins"—*Good News Bible*
"Leave your evil ways and turn to God"—*Living Bible*

4. ORIGINAL WORD AND SHORT DEFINITION

- "metanoeo" (Greek), "to change one's mind"
- "metamelomai" (Greek), "to regret or show remorse"

───────── WORD STUDY FORM ─────────

5. OCCURRENCES IN THE BIBLE

Two different Greek words are translated "repent" in the New Testament:

A. *Metanoeo*

"Repent" (verb), 34 times   "Repentance" (noun), 24 times

     5 times in Matthew   3 times in Matthew
     2 times in Mark   2 times in Mark
     9 times in Luke   5 times in Luke
     5 times in Acts   6 times in Acts
     1 time in 2 Corinthians   1 time in Romans
     12 times in Revelation   2 times in 2 Corinthians
                            1 time in 2 Timothy
                            3 times in Hebrews
                            1 time in 2 Peter

B. *Metamelomai*

"Repent" (verb) — 6 times

     3 times in Matthew
     2 times in 2 Corinthians
     1 time in Hebrews

Interesting Insights

- The word is never used in the gospel of John; but it is used in Revelation 12 times.
- The author Luke used it the most (Luke and Acts).
- Repentance is not emphasized much in the Epistles because they were written to believers.

— WORD STUDY FORM —

6. ROOT MEANING AND ORIGIN   (use reference books)

Metanoeo literally means "to perceive afterward." It is made up of two Greek words: *meta*, which means "after" (implying change), and *noeo*, which means "to perceive" (*nous* is Greek for "the mind").

From this we get the meaning of "to change one's mind or purpose." In the New Testament this change is always for the better, and it denotes a genuine, complete change of heart and life.

Not only does it imply a turning away (negative) from sin, but a turning to (positive) that which is right and godly. It means more than just feeling sorry for wrong you've done. It also means to completely change your mind about the sin and go a different way.

Metamelomai comes from *meta* ("after") and *melo* ("to care for"). It means to regret or express remorse for something you wish you hadn't done. It means to have painful anxiety (sorrow) over a past deed. This is *not* genuine repentance. It means to regret something you did without ever really changing your mind about it. ("I'm sorry I got caught, but I'm not sorry I did it." Or "I'm not sure I wouldn't do it again.") The best illustration of this is Judas. He was regretful for betraying Jesus (*metamelomai*—Matt. 27:3), but he never genuinely repented of it (*metanoeo*).

—————— WORD STUDY FORM ——————

7. HOW THE WORD WAS USED

A. In Other Writings:

Metanoeo was not used much in classical Greek literature. When the word was used, it did not mean the radical change of a person's life as a whole as it does in the New Testament.

B. Throughout the Bible:

- Repentance (*nâham*) in the Old Testament is seen most clearly in Ezekiel 18 and 33:10–20.
- "Repent" was the basic message of John the Baptist (Matt. 3:2), Jesus (Matt. 4:17), the 12 disciples (Mark 6:12), Peter at Pentecost (Acts 2:38).
- It is commanded by God for everyone (Acts 17:30; 2 Peter 3:9).
- It is part of saving faith (Luke 13:5; Acts 3:19).
- It produces joy in heaven (Luke 15:7, 10).
- It is proven by our actions (Acts 26:20).
- Jesus used the word 17 times in the Gospels and 8 times in Revelation.
- What causes us to repent?
  —God's goodness to us (Rom. 2:4)
  —Godly sorrow for our sin (2 Cor. 7:9–10)
  —God's grace (2 Tim. 2:25)
- It is a foundational truth of the Christian life (Heb. 6:1).

C. In the Context of the Passage: 2 Corinthians 7:9–10

This verse shows the difference between genuine repentance (*metanoeo*) and mere regret (*metamelomai*). Real godly sorrow brings about genuine repentance. This brings about a change of life, not just regret.

—————— WORD STUDY FORM ——————

8. APPLICATION

"Or do you show contempt for the riches of his kindness, forbearance, and patience, not realizing that God's kindness is intended to lead you to repentance?" (Rom. 2:4)

Sin to Confess/Attitude to Change

I have held a personal grudge in my heart against John ever since the incident in the mountains last fall. It has put a strain on our relationship. The Lord has convicted me about this in the past, but I have put off making restitution. I know I have sinned. I want to repent of this sin now. Tomorrow afternoon I will go to John and ask his forgiveness. I want to straighten this matter out.

RESOURCE BOOKS USED

New International Dictionary of New Testament Theology, Vol. 1
Vine's Expository Dictionary of New Testament Words
Young's Analytical Concordance to the Bible

WORD STUDY FORM

1. ENGLISH WORD

2. ENGLISH DEFINITION

3. COMPARISON OF TRANSLATIONS

4. ORIGINAL WORD AND SHORT DEFINITION

RICK WARREN'S BIBLE STUDY METHODS

WORD STUDY FORM

5. OCCURRENCES IN THE BIBLE

156

WORD STUDY FORM

6. ROOT MEANING AND ORIGIN (use reference books)

WORD STUDY FORM

7. HOW THE WORD WAS USED

A. In Other Writings:

B. Throughout the Bible:

C. In the Context of the Passage:

WORD STUDY FORM

8. APPLICATION

RESOURCE BOOKS USED

THE BOOK BACKGROUND METHOD OF BIBLE STUDY

8

How to Research Biblical Backgrounds

It is much easier to understand and appreciate a play if all the props and background scenes are in place. The actors on the stage perform against the backdrop of the props and painted scenery. It is the same way with Scripture. God's revelation was given in the midst of history, and the *dramatis personae* of the Bible act out their God-given roles against the background of their times. We understand the Word of God more clearly when we see it against the backdrop of the days in which it was written.

DEFINITION

The Book Background Method of Bible Study involves gaining a better understanding of the biblical message by researching the background related to the passage, person, event, or topic being studied. This involves understanding the geography, historical events, culture, and political environment at the time a particular part of the Bible was written.

WHY STUDY BACKGROUNDS?

In order to get the full impact of what a biblical writer is saying, it is necessary to "transport" ourselves back into the time in which he lived. Since we are centuries removed from Bible times, we must try to see their world through their eyes, feel what they felt, and then understand how the Holy Spirit of God used them to write what they did.

One of the primary rules of interpretation states that since the Bible was written in the midst of history, it can only be understood more fully in light of that history. You cannot interpret the Bible correctly if you ignore the influence of the times in which it was written. Serious Bible students will always want to know the geographical, historical, cultural, and political backgrounds of the passage or book they are studying.

Furthermore, before we can understand the way we are to apply the message to us today, we must first be sure how it was applied during the time it was first written. If we try to interpret and apply Scripture according to our own age and culture, we will quickly run into many difficulties. Often a statement, word, custom, or event in another culture or time will be understood in a sense totally different from the meaning we attach to it today in our country.

Because of the tremendous archaeological discoveries in the past century, we now have a much better understanding of the cultures and historical backgrounds of biblical times. Most of this information is available through excellent research tools. You will definitely have to consult these when you do this method of Bible study.

THE VALUE OF ARCHAEOLOGY

To many people archaeology is a dry, boring, and little-known science. But thanks to the patient work of many skilled archaeologists of many nations, we know much more today about Bible times than

STEP ONE — *Choose the Subject or Book of the Bible*

STEP TWO — *List Your Reference Tools*

STEP THREE — *Obtain Insights from Geography*

STEP FOUR — *Get Insights from History*

STEP FIVE — *Discover Some Insights from Culture*

STEP SIX — *Research Insights from the Political Environment*

STEP SEVEN — *Summarize Your Research*

STEP EIGHT — *Write Out a Personal Application*

Christians did even half a century ago. *National Geographic* and other popular magazines have publicized such findings as the Ebla tablets, which throw tremendous light on the Near East of 2000 to 2500 B.C. We can understand the Bible today as never before, as archaeology has been a great enlightener and friend to the serious Bible student. Gus W. Van Beek has written,

> No one can understand the Bible without a knowledge of biblical history and culture, and no one can claim a knowledge of biblical history and culture without an understanding of the contributions of archaeology. Biblical events have been illustrated, obscure words defined, ideas explained, and chronology refined by archaeological finds. To say that our knowledge of the Bible has been revolutionized by these discoveries is almost to understate the facts ("Archaeology," *Interpreter's Dictionary of the Bible* [Abingdon Press, 1962], 1:203).

TOOLS YOU WILL NEED

This method of Bible study is totally dependent on tools, so you will have to obtain some of these or borrow them from your public or church library. Don't be afraid of them. Instead, take advantage of the information that scholars have spent their lives finding out for you. The following tools will provide helpful background material:

- A Bible dictionary and/or Bible encyclopedia
- A Bible handbook
- A Bible atlas

In addition, you may want to consult some of the following reference books that deal with the geography, history, culture, and everyday life of Bible times.

- *Archaeology and Bible History* by Joseph Free and Howard Vos (Zondervan)
- *The Bible and Archaeology* by J. A. Thompson (Eerdmans)
- *Everyday Life in Bible Times* (National Geographic Society)
- *Great People of the Bible and How They Lived* (Reader's Digest Association)
- *Harper's Encyclopedia of Bible Life* by Madeleine S. and J. Lane Miller (Book Sales)
- *The Oxford History of the Biblical World* by Michael Coogan (Oxford University Press)
- *The Wycliffe Historical Geography of Bible Lands* by Howard Vos (Hendrickson)

This is only a representative list, for many other reference works are available today. Visit your local public library, your church library, or your local Christian bookstore and look over what they have. Choose the ones that appeal to you the most. Archaeologists are constantly updating their findings through new discoveries, so be sure to obtain the latest edition of each reference tool.

SIMPLE STEPS ON DOING A BACKGROUND STUDY

The Book Background Study Form has eight steps plus some blank space for listing the reference tools you use. Use additional sheets of paper if you do not have room on the form.

STEP ONE *Choose the Subject or Book of the Bible*

Choose the subject, person, word, or book of the Bible you want to study, and begin gathering reference materials for your research. The availability of reference tools will largely determine the scope of your study.

STEP TWO *List Your Reference Tools*

List all the reference tools you have gathered to do this study (see "Tools You Will Need" above). This is to help you remember which books were most useful for the background material you researched and what books you may want to refer to in future background studies.

STEP THREE *Obtain Insights from Geography*

You will need to become familiar with the geography of Palestine and the Near East in general. This includes the types of land found there, the major mountains and hills, elevation and rainfall, the major bodies of water (seas, lakes, rivers), location of cities and countries, famous landmarks, and the borders of surrounding countries of the time you are studying.

As you study the New Testament, particularly Paul's missionary travels, you will need to become acquainted with the Mediterranean countries and cities that were active during the days of the Roman Empire.

In all of your study of biblical geography, you must continually ask this question: "What is the effect of the surrounding geography on what I am studying?"

In this step, list all the insights you can get on geography for the subject or book you are studying.

STEP FOUR   *Get Insights from History*

You should have a working knowledge of the chronology (order of historical events) of the nation of Israel in the Old Testament. Learn the periods of history of the Hebrew nation; find out the origin and history of famous cities; learn the divisions of Jesus' ministry; be well versed on the history surrounding Paul's missionary travels. It is also helpful to know what major events were going on in other parts of the world during the time you are studying, in order to have a proper perspective on what God was doing in the world.

You might ask yourself, "What caused this particular event that I am studying? How did it affect the people involved? How did it affect the passage I am studying?" Be especially aware of events that illustrate God's sovereign control over the progress of history.

In this step, list all the insights you can get on the history surrounding the subject or book you are studying.

STEP FIVE   *Discover Some Insights from Culture*

If you are to understand what went on in Bible times, you need to learn about the total lifestyle of the ancient people in the Scriptures. Here are some areas you can research while asking yourself, "How do all these things affect the message and the people about whom I am studying?"

- Types of clothing people wore
- Professions and trades in biblical times
- Music in the Bible
- Architectural styles in the Near East
- Manners and customs in Scripture
- Recreation in ancient times
- Family life in the Middle East
- Art in the Bible
- Languages and literature of surrounding nations

- Religious ceremonies in Israel and among pagan neighbors
- False religions of the area
- Weapons and tools used by the people

In this step, list all the insights you derive from the way people lived in their cultures.

STEP SIX *Research Insights from the Political Environment*

Much of what happened in Israel in the Old Testament and in the Roman world of Jesus, Paul, and the apostles is related to the political environment of the times. Kings, emperors, rulers, and other powers governed the people of the time. Israel, for example, spent much of its history under foreign rule and even in exile. These other nations and political systems were bound to have an effect on the way God's people lived. Recognize, however, that God is always in control of the political situation. Even King Nebuchadnezzar acknowledged this fact (Dan. 4:34 – 35).

Egypt, Philistia, Assyria, Babylon, Persia, Greece, and Rome all played a major part in the Bible. What were these nations like? How did they affect Israel or the New Testament church? Many of the prophets' messages can only be understood in light of their current political climate.

In this step, write down all the insights you can from your research into the political conditions of the time period you are studying.

STEP SEVEN *Summarize Your Research*

Now go back over Steps Three through Six, and from the data you have gathered, summarize your research by answering these two questions:

- How does this background information help me understand better what I am studying?
- What influence did any of these factors have on the subject (or book) that I am studying?

| STEP EIGHT | *Write Out a Personal Application* |

Although a personal application may be hard to come by in this type of study, you should be able to get one from your original subject. In fact, research into the background of your subject may enable you to find an application you may need today, and the data can help you make that application personally relevant.

HOW TO FILL IN THE BOOK BACKGROUND STUDY FORM

The form at the end of this chapter should help you in this study, or you may mark your own paper with the divisions suggested on the form.

Filling Out the Form

Follow the steps just outlined and write in the insights gleaned from your research. Then summarize the insights in Step Seven. If you need more room, use the back of the form or another sheet of paper.

Sample Filled-out Form

See the example on Ephesus at the end of this chapter.

Assignment

Some subjects to consider as you begin using the Book Background Study Method are

- The book of Philippians
- The book of Haggai
- The book of Colossians
- The book of Ruth
- Pharisees and Sadducees

- Temple worship
- The Romans in Palestine

For Further Reading

The books listed under "Tools You Will Need" are excellent for getting started on this method. For some methodology or "how-to" hints, you may read "The Historical Method" in Merrill C. Tenney's *Galatians: The Charter of Christian Liberty* (Eerdmans), pages 97 – 109. Here are some additional resources:

The Bible Knowledge Background Commentary, edited by Craig Evans, 3 vols. (Victor)

Chronological and Background Charts of the New Testament by H. Wayne House (Zondervan)

Chronological and Background Charts of the Old Testament by John Walton (Zondervan)

The IVP Bible Background Commentary: New Testament by Craig Keener (InterVarsity Press)

The IVP Bible Background Commentary: Old Testament by John Walton et al. (InterVarsity Press)

Manners and Customs in the Bible by Victor H. Matthews (Hendrickson)

Zondervan Illustrated Bible Backgrounds Commentary: New Testament, edited by Clinton Arnold, 12 vols. (Zondervan)

Zondervan Illustrated Bible Backgrounds Commentary: Old Testament, edited by John Walton, 5 vols. (Zondervan)

——— BOOK BACKGROUND STUDY FORM ———

1. SUBJECT Ephesus (Book of Ephesians)

2. REFERENCE TOOLS USED

Eerdmans Handbook to the Bible
New Bible Dictionary
The Zondervan Encyclopedia of the Bible

3. GEOGRAPHICAL BACKGROUND

The city was situated on the western coast of Asia Minor at the mouth of the Cayster River, one of the four major east-west valleys that ended in the Aegean Sea. It was at the beginning of a major highway that went eastward across Asia Minor into Syria, then into Mesopotamia, Persia, and India.

Ephesus was a large port city and had a population of around 400,000 in the apostle Paul's time. It was the most important city in the Roman province of Asia. Its strategic location caused it to be the meeting place of the land and sea trade routes in that part of the world in those days.

RICK WARREN'S BIBLE STUDY METHODS

BOOK BACKGROUND STUDY FORM

4. HISTORICAL BACKGROUND

Ephesus was an ancient city whose origins are lost in the mists of antiquity. It was known as an important port city in the days of the ancient Hittites (early 1300s B.C.).

Around 1080 B.C. it was taken and colonized by the Greeks from across the Aegean Sea, and Greek ways and influences were introduced. Five centuries later it was taken by the legendary King Croesus, who restored Asian influence to the city.

The Persians took Ephesus in 557 B.C., and two centuries of conflict with the Greeks over it followed. Alexander the Great captured the city in 335 B.C., and the Greek influence prevailed until Roman times.

The Romans took the city in 190 B.C., and it remained in their hands or their allies' hands until after the days of Paul. It became the major city in the Roman province of Asia, although Pergamum remained the capital.

BOOK BACKGROUND STUDY FORM

5. CULTURAL BACKGROUND

From the time the Greeks took the city in 1080 B.C., cultural conflict existed between the Asian and Greek ways of life. The original religion included the worship of the mother-goddess whom the Greeks later called Artemis (Diana in the Roman system). Here the original goddess had a shrine, and the Greeks later built a grand temple that became known throughout the whole Mediterranean world.

Being at the crossroads of Europe and the Far East, the city had an international flavor as people of many backgrounds, particularly traders and sailors, mixed here freely. Thus it was a cosmopolitan city, primarily Greek in culture but with Asian underpinnings existing there at the same time. It had all the conveniences of a modern Roman city—gymnasium, stadium, theaters, and central marketplace.

6. POLITICAL BACKGROUND

In Paul's day, since it was a city loyal to Rome, Ephesus was governed by the Roman proconsul from Pergamum. It was allowed to have its own government and was divided into "tribes" according to the ethnic composition of its population. In Paul's time there were six tribes, and the representatives to their gathering elected the "town clerk," who was responsible for all public meetings.

Other government officials included the Asiarchs, municipal officers of Rome, and the Neokoros, the temple officials.

BOOK BACKGROUND STUDY FORM

7. SUMMARY OF INSIGHTS

The city of Ephesus was an important city, and because of its strategic value, Paul and his team headed there on their second missionary journey. Paul later ministered there for some time on his third journey.

Because of its cosmopolitan population, here was an opportunity for ministry to many different kinds of peoples—Romans, Greeks, and the Asians of that part of Asia. Also, a ministry could be had with the travelers and traders, who came both by land and by sea.

Ephesus' history and geography made the city strategic for the planting of churches and then the spreading of the news of the gospel throughout the whole territory around it as well as to many other places through the caravans and shipping.

8. PERSONAL APPLICATION

In a day of population explosion it is my responsibility to witness to Jesus Christ in the strategic places of the world. This means that in my town I need to find out where the strategic centers of people gathering are. Then I should plan to go there, both by myself and with my church, to testify to the grace of God and his salvation. I will talk with Sam and Joe about this, and we will lay plans together for evangelizing our community.

BOOK BACKGROUND STUDY FORM

1. SUBJECT

2. REFERENCE TOOLS USED

3. GEOGRAPHICAL BACKGROUND

RICK WARREN'S BIBLE STUDY METHODS

BOOK BACKGROUND STUDY FORM

4. HISTORICAL BACKGROUND

BOOK BACKGROUND STUDY FORM

5. CULTURAL BACKGROUND

6. POLITICAL BACKGROUND

BOOK BACKGROUND STUDY FORM

7. SUMMARY OF INSIGHTS

8. PERSONAL APPLICATION

9

THE BOOK SURVEY
METHOD OF
BIBLE STUDY

How to Get an Overview of a Bible Book

Martin Luther, who began the great Reformation in the 16th century, not only restored the Bible to the common people, but also gave some practical suggestions for Bible study. He once said that he studied the Scriptures the way he gathered apples: "First I shake the whole Apple tree [study of the Bible as a whole], that the ripest might fall. Then I climb the tree and shake each limb [study of a whole book], and then each branch [study of a chapter of a book] and then each twig [study of the paragraphs and sentences], and then I look under each leaf [study of single words]."

The next three chapters go together because the three methods discussed are really part of one. They are three steps in studying a book of the Bible. When combined, these three methods give you the most comprehensive approach to studying the Word of God. They may require extra work, effort, and time, but they can reward you with the greatest results.

Because God gave his revelation in segments that we call books, we should first study these books as a whole, then examine their parts carefully, and finally put our study together to see the whole again. So the approach we will be using is *survey, analysis,* and *synthesis.*

STEP ONE — *Read the Book*

STEP TWO — *Make Notes on What You Read*

STEP THREE — *Do a Background Study*

STEP FOUR — *Make a Horizontal Chart of the Book's Contents*

STEP FIVE — *Make a Tentative Outline of the Book*

STEP SIX — *Write Out a Personal Application*

First, we make an initial survey of the book to see it as a whole; this is our "telescopic view" study. Then we take the book apart chapter by chapter and do a detailed analysis of each one; we look at all the details as through a microscope. Finally, we put it all together again in a synthetic study in which we summarize the book as a whole and produce *our own* outline. The process moves from the whole to the particulars and back to the whole:

- *Survey*—get a bird's-eye view of the book.
- *Analysis*—study everything in each chapter in detail.
- *Synthesis*—put it back together again and draw some conclusions.

Note: These three methods have been developed effectively by the Navigators in their collegiate ministry. The three steps have been combined by them into the Comprehensive Book Analysis Method, which is explained and illustrated in depth in *The Navigator Bible Studies Handbook* (NavPress).

Chapters 9–11 in this book present only what the Comprehensive Book Analysis does not deal with and will suggest some alternative approaches from the book published by the Navigators. (Theirs is highly recommended for those who have done extensive chapter analysis Bible study and would like a slightly different approach.)

We look first at part one of this process: the Book Survey Method.

DEFINITION

A book survey study involves gaining a sweeping overview of an entire book of the Bible. It is taking a "skyscraper look" or a "telescopic view" of a book by reading it through several times without stopping to consider the details. Then you ask a series of background and content questions and draw a horizontal chart of its contents in order to gain a general understanding of the writer's purpose, theme, structure, and content.

WHY THIS METHOD OF BIBLE STUDY

As you know, the Bible is really 66 different books compiled under one cover. Each book is unique and has an important message for us today. The Book Survey Method is a practical way to master the general contents of a single book.

ITS IMPORTANCE

Doing a book survey as the first part of an analysis and synthesis helps reveal how each part of the book is related to the other parts. Many verses that are hard to understand become clear when seen in the larger context of the book in which they are found. And the place of a verse in a book is often the key to understanding it and what God teaches through it.

Doing a book survey first also reveals the proper emphasis of each point in the book. It keeps the study of God's Word balanced, lessening the possibility of overemphasizing or minimizing any one point. It is interesting that most cults and heresies have arisen throughout history when people overemphasize some verse or doctrine and build their whole theology on a few verses taken out of context while ignoring much of the rest of God's revelation.

TOOLS YOU WILL NEED

A number of basic tools (discussed in the Introduction) are necessary for this method of Bible study. These helpful tools are

- A study Bible.
- Several contemporary translations. (These enable you to see different renderings of the same material by able scholars.)
- A Bible dictionary and/or Bible encyclopedia.
- A Bible handbook. (Look under the name of the book you are studying as well as under the writer and the city or people to whom the original might have been sent.)

In addition to the above basic tools, you may want to consult Bible atlases, historical geographies, historical background books, and Bible surveys. Use these last tools only after you have done your own research. Later you may check yourself and your conclusions against what other reliable scholars have done. There are many surveys and background books to choose from:

- *The Illustrated Guide to Biblical History* by Kendall Easley (Broadman & Holman)

- *Nelson's New Testament Survey* by Mark Bailey and Tom Constable (Nelson)
- *Nelson's Old Testament Survey* by Charles Dyer and Eugene Merrill (Nelson)
- *New Testament Survey* by Merrill C. Tenney (Eerdmans)
- *New Testament Times* by Merrill C. Tenney (Baker)
- *The Old Testament Speaks* by Samuel J. Schultz (HarperSanFrancisco)
- *Old Testament Times* by R. K. Harrison (Baker)
- *Old Testament Today* by John Walton and Andrew Hill (Zondervan)
- *Survey of the Bible* by William Hendriksen (Baker)
- *A Survey of the New Testament* by Robert H. Gundry (Zondervan)
- *What the Bible Is All About: NIV Edition* by Henrietta C. Mears (Regal)

You must recognize that these Bible surveys, like Bible commentaries, represent the opinions and theological positions of their authors. So select the one or two that best suit you, and use them after you have done your own initial survey study.

SIMPLE STEPS ON DOING A SURVEY STUDY

The Book Survey Study Form has many parts, which fit under the six steps for doing this study. One step will be done on a separate sheet of paper.

STEP ONE *Read the Book*

This first step may seem obvious, but some people spend all their time reading *about* the Bible rather than reading the Scripture text itself. The only tools needed for this first step are your study Bible and several recent translations. *Do not read any Bible surveys, handbooks, or commentaries at this point.* Follow these seven suggestions:

1. *Read through the book at one sitting.* Except for the Psalms, the longest book in the Bible is Isaiah, and it can be read in three or four hours. Most of the other books, particularly those in the New Testament, can be read in much less time. If you have to break up your reading, try to finish a book in no more than two sittings. (For example, read Isaiah 1–39 at one sitting, then Isaiah 40–66.) You will be amazed at what you begin to see in Scripture as you do this.

2. *Read through the book in a recent translation.* This will enable you to understand what you are reading better, because you will be doing your reading in contemporary language.

3. *Read through the book rapidly, ignoring the chapter divisions.* Remember that the chapter divisions and verses were not in the original writing; they were added much later for convenience. Right now your purpose is to get the flow of the book and feel the pulse of the writer. Don't be concerned with the details at this stage (you will do that in the Chapter Analysis Method, chap. 10), but read the book quickly to get its main thrust.

4. *Read through the book repeatedly.* Repeat the process of reading as many times as you can. (Obviously, you will not be able to read the book of Isaiah as many times as the book of Colossians in a given time frame.) Each time you read the book through, you will notice some new things and the overall picture will become clearer and clearer. The more times you read a book through, the better you will be able to understand it. So stay with it.

5. *Read through the book without referring to commentaries or someone else's notes.* It is good to read in a Bible in which you have not made any notes yourself. Otherwise, when you see the notes you may have written (your own or others'), your mind will naturally fall back into that pattern and you will be hindered from seeing new things. After you have finished Step One, you may begin consulting reference helps.

6. *Read through the book prayerfully.* Ask God to speak to your heart and open your eyes that you may see wonderful things in his law (Ps. 119:18).

7. *Read through the book with pen or pencil in hand.* As you begin reading the second or third time through, begin taking notes and making observations on what you are reading (see Step Two and the Book Survey Form).

STEP TWO *Make Notes on What You Read*

As you read through the book (see Step One), write down your impressions and the important facts you discover. Make these notes on a separate piece of paper or on the Book Survey Form found at the end of this chapter. Look for the following nine items:

1. *Category:* Is the book history? Poetry? Prophecy? Law? A biography? A letter?
2. *First Impressions:* What is the first impression you get from the book? What do you think is the purpose of the writer? What "feel" do you get from reading it?
3. *Key Words:* What are some of the significant words the writer uses? What words are repeated the most? What word or words is he emphasizing?
4. *Key Verse:* What seems to be the key verse (if any)? What ideas or phrases are repeated that may show his main thought? What is the writer's key statement?
5. *Literary Style:* Is the book a narrative? A drama? A personal letter? A discourse? Poetry? A combination of narration and poetry? Does the writer use figurative speech? Is he using a logical argument?
6. *Emotional Tone:* Is the writer angry? Sad? Happy? Worried? Excited? Depressed? Calm? How do you think his

hearers must have felt when they received this writing? How does it make *you* feel?

7. *Main Theme(s):* What is the main theme? Is there more than one? What is the writer saying? What is his major emphasis?

8. *Structure:* Are there obvious divisions of thought in the book? How is the book organized? Around people? Events? Places? Ideas? Time spans?

9. *Major People:* Who are the principal personalities in the book? Which people are mentioned the most, and what parts do they play in the book?

STEP THREE   *Do a Background Study*

Find out the historical and geographical setting of the book. Into what background does the book fit? You can use the following questions to help you find some of the facts. Also use the ideas presented in the Book Background Method of Bible Study (chap. 8). Many of the answers may be found right in the book itself, so look there first. If you can't find the answers in the text alone, then check outside references (see "Tools You Will Need" earlier in this chapter).

- What can I learn about the writer(s)?
- When was the book written? (Date)
- Where was the book written?
- To whom was the book written? Who were they? Who was he? Who was she? (Find out about their historical and geographical backgrounds.)
- Why was the book written? (Investigate the circumstances related to the writing.)
- What other background information sheds light on this book?
- What is the place of this book in the Bible? Is it a bridge between various periods of history?

- What are the geographic locations mentioned in the book? Where are they? (Draw a map if it will be helpful to you.)

| STEP FOUR | *Make a Horizontal Chart of the Book's Contents* |

One of the exciting steps in doing a book survey is making a horizontal chart. This is a diagrammed layout of a book's contents on one or two sheets of paper. The value of such a chart is that it enables you to lay out visually the book's contents and divisions. It gives you a new perspective of the book. The three parts of a simple horizontal chart are the *major divisions* of the book, *chapter titles,* and *paragraph titles.*

Why make a horizontal chart? You gain several benefits in this study by making one.

- It helps you summarize the main ideas and contents of a book.
- It enables you to see the contents of an entire book at a glance.
- It helps you discover the relationships between chapters and between paragraphs.
- It makes you aware of ideas repeated in several places in the book.
- It serves as a memory device to help you recall a chapter's content quickly.
- It enables you to think through a book and remember it.

Preparation for making a horizontal chart. You need three tools to make a simple horizontal chart:

- A Bible with paragraph divisions. Many recent versions have divided the text into paragraphs to enable you to see the units of thought. You have to know these in order to make the chart.
- A pencil (or pen) and a ruler.
- A blank sheet of paper, preferably 8½ x 11 inches in size. Try to fit your chart on one sheet of paper so you can see the entire structure of the book at a glance. When you are

working on a long book (e.g., Isaiah, Genesis, Psalms), try to use as few sheets as possible. In using more than one sheet, be sure to use the same scale so you can match the sheets.

How to make a horizontal chart. Go through the following four steps for each chart you make.

1. On a blank sheet of paper, make as many vertical columns as there are chapters in the book. For longer books, make the columns narrower and abbreviate what you write in them and use two or three sheets of paper as needed.

2. Read through the book again and find its *major divisions.* Record these divisions in as few words as possible at the top of your chart (see the sample filled-out form).

3. Read through the book again and think of a *title for each chapter* (or group of chapters in a longer book). Record these at the top of each column directly below the major divisions. Irving Jensen has suggested five characteristics of good chapter titles (*Independent Bible Study,* Moody Press, p. 108).

- Preferably use one word, not more than four.
- Use picturesque words that help you visualize the contents.
- Use words taken directly from the text if possible.
- Use words that have not been used previously as chapter titles in your study of other books.
- Use words that tell you where you are in the book.

4. Read through the book once more and do the same thing to all the paragraphs in your book. Try to relate the *paragraph titles* to the chapter title under which they fall.

As you become proficient in this exercise, you may add things to your charts that personalize your study.

STEP FIVE   *Make a Tentative Outline of the Book*

After you have summarized the contents of the book on a horizontal chart, you are ready to make a simple tentative outline of the book. Later on, in the Book Synthesis Method of Bible Study (chap. 11), you will make your final, detailed outline of the book. In the current method you should merely outline the high points of the book and show their relationship with one another. Here are some suggestions:

1. Refer to your horizontal chart for ideas in outlining. Often your chart will readily show the natural organization of the book's contents.

2. Outline from the major to the minor. Look for major divisions of the book first, then the subdivisions (which could be the chapters themselves), and finally the important points that fall under the subdivisions (which could be the paragraphs). In longer books you may need to have further subpoints under these.

3. Watch your paragraph divisions for clues in outlining. Since the paragraph is the basic unit of thought in writing, you can use the paragraph divisions as a guide in designing the outline of the chapter. Write a summary statement for each paragraph, then use those statements as the major points of your outline.

4. After you have done your own outlining, compare yours with as many other outlines as you can. Check the reference books available to you and compare your work with those writers. Don't be concerned if your outline does not match these exactly, for often there are many ways to outline a book. You will discover that even notable scholars disagree with each other.

STEP SIX   *Write Out a Personal Application*

Even though the main purpose of a book survey is to get you acquainted with its general contents, you should not forget to make a personal application of some insight you discover along the way.

Select one thing the Lord spoke to you about from your survey and write a personal, practical, possible, and measurable application on that truth. (See the instructions in chapter 1 on how to write a meaningful application.)

HOW TO FILL IN THE BOOK SURVEY FORM

Use the form at the end of this chapter or draft divisions on your own sheet of paper.

Filling Out the Form

You will use this form or your own sheet with the divisions plus another sheet (for the horizontal chart). Write out the name of the book in the blank provided and the number of chapters the book contains. Then follow the six steps discussed above, with the nine items listed under Step Two.

1. Record the total number of times you have read through the book.
2. From your various readings, fill in the sections on your blank Book Survey Form. Refer back to Step Two, "Make Notes on What You Read."
3. Record whatever background observations you believe help you understand this book.
4. On a separate piece of paper, draw a simple horizontal chart.
5. In outline form write out a summary or overview of the book.
6. Write out one practical application.

Sample Filled-out Form

See the example on the book of Ephesians at the end of this chapter.

Assignment

Begin your study of books of the Bible — Book Survey, Chapter Analysis, Book Synthesis — with some of the shorter epistles of the New Testament. Once you have mastered the process, you may want to try Mark, the shortest gospel, or one of the shorter minor prophets. Here is a suggested order in which to begin:

- 1 Thessalonians
- 1 John
- Philippians
- 2 Timothy
- Ephesians
- Mark
- Romans
- Habakkuk

After doing these, select your own books to study.

For Further Reading

In addition to the following books, see the surveys and background books suggested under "Tools You Will Need" earlier in this chapter.

How to Read the Bible Book by Book by Gordon Fee and Douglas Stuart (Zondervan)

Independent Bible Study by Irving L. Jensen (Moody Press)

A Literary Guide to the Bible by Leland Ryken and Tremper Longman (Zondervan)

The Navigator Bible Studies Handbook (NavPress)

Studying, Interpreting, and Applying the Bible by Walter A. Henrichsen and Gayle Jackson (Zondervan)

——— BOOK SURVEY FORM ———

BOOK Ephesians   **CHAPTERS** 6

1. NUMBER OF TIMES READ 5

2. NOTES ON THE BOOK

- **Category:** New Testament letter

- **First Impressions:** It is a book that strengthens my faith and challenges me to my responsibilities. Strongly doctrinal.

- **Key Words:** "in Christ" and "walk" (KJV)

- **Key Verse:** 1:3 and 4:1

- **Literary Style:** A general letter that is punctuated by two worshipful prayers.

- **Emotional Tone:** Calm with the intention of teaching the readers and challenging them to their responsibilities.

- **Main Theme(s):** What we are because of Jesus Christ ("in Christ") and the responsibilities that are ours because of our standing.

- **Structure:** Two main divisions separated by a "therefore." In the first part, two prayers are recorded.

- **Major People:** Paul, the Ephesian church, evil forces, and Tychicus

REFERENCE BOOKS USED

Eerdmans Handbook to the Bible
William Hendriksen's *Ephesians*
New Bible Dictionary

BOOK SURVEY FORM

3. BACKGROUND OF BOOK

Paul had founded the church in Ephesus on his second missionary journey and left Priscilla and Aquila there to follow up with the converts. There they had an influence on Apollos's life.

At the beginning of his third mission, Paul returned and ministered in the city for a lengthy time, during which the gospel spread throughout all of the province of Asia.

Then, after Paul was imprisoned in Rome, he wrote a letter to this church. Its occasion was simply an opportunity to strengthen the church both doctrinally and practically. It was written to reinforce believers there in their opinion of themselves (in light of the other powerful religious influences in the city—e.g., the temple of Artemis) and in carrying out their responsibilities as Christians in their community.

Many references in the book have pertinence to the original readers because the background is the city of Ephesus—its culture, government, and history. (See the Book Background Study for details on these.)

4. HORIZONTAL CHART

Who the Members of the Church Are 1:1 – 3:21			What the Members of the Church Are to Do 4:1 – 6:24		
Chosen by God	Saved by Christ	Empowered by the Holy Spirit	Responsibilities	Relationships	Conflict
1	2	3	4:1 – 5:21	5:22 – 6:9	6:10 – 20
Three doxologies separate the work of the Trinity: • Father (1:4 – 6) • Son (1:7 – 12) • Holy Spirit (1:13 – 14)	The work of Christ is seen as a work of grace that we receive by faith. • Redemption (2:1 – 10) • Reconciliation (2:11 – 22) (The results of each are seen here.)	The ministry of the Holy Spirit is to make all believers of all backgrounds one in Christ. This was a mystery before.	"Therefore ..." 1. We are to have a united walk (4:1 – 16). 2. We are to have an understanding walk (4:17 – 32). 3. We are to have a holy walk (5:1 – 14). 4. We are to have a Spirit-led walk (5:15 – 21).	The specifics are now given: 1. Husbands and wives (5:22 – 33) 2. Parents and children (6:1 – 4) 3. "Employer" and "employee" (6:5 – 9)	The reason we have difficulties in our responsibilities and relationships is our spiritual warfare. But we have God's armor to protect us.
Paul's first prayer (1:15 – 23)		Paul's second prayer (3:14 – 21)		Paul's closing greetings; Tychicus sent (6:21 – 24)	

BOOK SURVEY FORM

5. TENTATIVE OUTLINE OF THE BOOK

I. Who the Members of the Church Are (1–3)
   A. They have been chosen by God (1) (ends with a prayer)
   B. They have been saved by Christ (2)
   C. They are empowered by the Holy Spirit (3) (ends with a prayer)
II. What the Members of the Church Are to Do (4–6)
   A. Their responsibilities (4:1–5:21)
   B. Their relationships at three levels (5:22–6:9)
   C. Their conflict with satanic powers (6:10–20)
Concluding remarks (6:21–24)

6. PERSONAL APPLICATION

What strikes me about this book is the close relationship between believing and acting. If I believe in Jesus Christ, then I am supposed to act in a Christian way. Because of who I am in the sight of God, certain actions are required of me in all my relationships.

Because I have been reconciled to others (chap. 2), I am to be forgiving in the same way Christ forgave me (4:32). I have not always been that forgiving and have held grudges and resentments. I will search my heart and make sure that I have forgiven everyone who may have "done me wrong"—real or imagined. Then, if necessary, I will go to these people and ask their forgiveness. As a check on myself, I will memorize Ephesians 4:32.

BOOK SURVEY FORM

BOOK	CHAPTERS

1. NUMBER OF TIMES READ

2. NOTES ON THE BOOK

- Category:

- First Impressions:

- Key Words:

- Key Verse:

- Literary Style:

- Emotional Tone:

- Main Theme(s):

- Structure:

- Major People:

REFERENCE BOOKS USED

BOOK SURVEY FORM

3. BACKGROUND OF BOOK

4. HORIZONTAL CHART

BOOK SURVEY FORM

5. TENTATIVE OUTLINE OF THE BOOK

6. PERSONAL APPLICATION

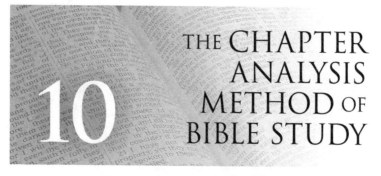

THE CHAPTER ANALYSIS METHOD OF BIBLE STUDY

How to Do an In-depth Study of a Chapter of a Bible Book

The second stage of studying a book of the Bible is to do a chapter analysis of each of the chapters of that book. After the survey study has been completed and you have a pretty good grasp and overview of the book, begin examining its individual parts. Since most chapter divisions are suitable and useful, it is best to examine the parts in this way.

DEFINITION

Chapter analysis involves gaining a thorough understanding of the material of a chapter of a book by looking carefully at each paragraph, sentence, and word in an intensely detailed and systematic manner. The three parts of this method are a Chapter Summary, a Verse-by-Verse Analysis, and a Chapter Conclusion. These parts may be done on the given form or on blank pieces of paper.

WHY DO A CHAPTER ANALYSIS?

Chapter Analysis, when done along with the Book Survey and Book Synthesis methods, enables us to understand the Bible in the way in

STEP ONE — *Write Out a Chapter Summary*

STEP TWO — *List Your Observations*

STEP THREE — *Ask Interpretation Questions*

STEP FOUR — *Correlate Your Chapter with Other Scriptures*

STEP FIVE — *List Some Possible Applications*

STEP SIX — *Write Down Some Concluding Thoughts*

STEP SEVEN — *Write Out One Application*

which it was written — in whole books. It is also a method in which we use limited outside helps, thus enabling us to learn the Scriptures on our own.

Note: Dawson Trotman, founder and first president of the Navigators, believed that this method is the major means of a Christian's intake of the Word of God. Hundreds of men and women in the early days of the organization were trained to do chapter analysis and received by it a biblical education comparable to that available in Bible institutes and colleges. Since that time, a number of excellent books have been published that expand on this method in detail. If this method especially interests you, I suggest you obtain some of the books listed at the end of this chapter. They provide excellent additional insights into this popular study method.

SIMPLE STEPS FOR DOING A CHAPTER ANALYSIS STUDY

In this method you begin with an introduction (chapter summary), which is Step One, then do a verse-by-verse analysis (Steps Two through Five), and finish with a chapter conclusion (Steps Six and Seven).

STEP ONE   *Write Out a Chapter Summary*

You begin this step by reading and rereading the chapter many times. All you are doing here is making general observations on the chapter as a whole. After you have read it through several times, describe the general contents in one of the ways about to be described. Do not try to interpret what you see at this time, but merely aim to become familiar with the chapter. You may summarize it in one of the following ways:

1. *Paraphrase it.* The simplest way is just to rephrase the chapter in your own words. Summarize it in such a way that you could read your paraphrase to another person. You can check some recent paraphrase versions of the Bible for examples of this.

2. *Outline it.* Another simple way to summarize is through an outline that follows the paragraph divisions of the chapter. Give a title to each paragraph, then place some subpoints under each one.

3. *Rewrite it without the modifying clauses and phrases.* Use just the subjects, verbs, and objects in your summary. This is a great way to summarize some of Paul's writings, for example, where run-on sentences (especially in the King James Version) are hard to understand because of their complexity.

After you have completed your chapter summary, give a title to the chapter, using either your title from the book survey or a new one that occurred to you during this study.

STEP TWO *List Your Observations*

This step begins the verse-by-verse analysis of the chapter. You start with the activity of observation. In this step you are looking in detail at every sentence and word and then writing down everything you see. You are trying to answer the question, "What does it say?"

Before you can begin to interpret the meaning of a verse or passage, you must first look at what it actually says. The purpose of observation is to saturate yourself completely with the contents of a Bible passage. The mark of good Bible students is that they have trained themselves to observe things in the text that others overlook.

Overlooking biblical facts—reasons why. There are three reasons why we often overlook things and miss so much in the biblical text: (1) We rush through a passage too quickly. So we need to slow down and not indulge in speed-reading. (2) We don't write down our observations. Louis Agassiz, a 19th-century professor of zoology at Harvard who taught his students the art of observation, used to say, "A pencil is the best eye." We need to write down what we see, and then we will begin seeing more. (3) We give up too soon. The longer we squeeze a lemon, the more juice we get out of it—to a point. But unlike lemons, the Bible never goes dry. We can study a text a hundred times and never exhaust the riches that are in it. So we shouldn't give up too soon; rather, we should keep on looking—the longer the better.

Asking questions. As has already been discussed, the secret of good Bible study is learning to ask the right questions (see the Introduction to this book). The number of questions you can ask of a text of Scripture increases in proportion to your willingness to stick with it. As you continue growing in Bible study skills, the type and number of questions you ask will improve and you will be able to observe more and more. The key to good observations, then, is a combination of diligence, patience, asking many questions, and writing down everything you see.

To help you in your observations, appendix F lists 30 ideas from which you can select the ones that will suit your study.

STEP THREE *Ask Interpretative Questions*

After observing all you can in the passage under study, you are ready to move on to interpretation. This step involves asking questions about meaning, then trying to find answers to them. In this exercise you discover the biblical writer's purpose and message by uncovering what he means by his idea.

Interpretive questions include asking *what* or *why*. Some examples:

- Why did the writer say this?
- What is the meaning of _____?
- What is the significance of _____?
- What is the implication of _____?
- Why is this important?

You should be able to think of many other interpretive questions to ask. Never think that any question is too silly or dumb. Always write every question down on your form even though you may not find an answer to it. Later on, in studying another chapter, you may be able to answer it; if so, come back to this chapter's form and fill in the answer. Remember that the more questions you ask, the more you will draw out of the text.

Listing difficulties. When you are writing down your questions, it is a good idea to include any difficulties you have in understanding what is being said. Two common types are *personal difficulties*—questions you would like answered in the future, or items for future study, and *possible difficulties*—matters that don't bother you at this time, but would be good to study so you can help others who might be bothered by them.

Finding the right meaning of the text. After you have listed all your questions of interpretation, you need to start finding some answers. There are several ways to do this.

1. *Check the context.* You should always start here, for often the answers to your questions will be found in the verses preceding or following the text. Always interpret a passage in light of its context. To review the context, you may have to go back to your observations or your book survey to answer these questions:

- Who is speaking?
- Who is being spoken to?
- When is it being spoken?
- Where is it being spoken?
- What is the occasion or circumstance?
- What is the *main* subject of the message?
- Is the aim of what is being said revealed?
- What other background material clarifies this statement?

You can avoid a great deal of misinterpretation by first checking out the context of a verse.

2. *Define the words and phrases used.* You must interpret your text according to the correct and proper meaning of the words. Look up the important words in a Bible dictionary, word study set, or English dictionary.

3. *Study the grammar and structure of the sentences.* Sometimes a problem of interpretation can be cleared up by diagramming a sentence or by understanding what grammatical usage the writer intended in the paragraph.

4. *Compare several translations of the text.* Use different recent versions of the Bible to see how the various translators rendered a particular word, phrase, or paragraph.

5. *Study the background of the text.* Interpret your text in light of the historical, cultural, geographic, economic, social, and political backgrounds of the book, including the current events of that time. This shows

you the value of doing a book survey study before attempting a chapter analysis study. Use your reference tools to check on the background, the writer's purpose in writing the book, and other pertinent factors.

6. *Compare your text with other passages of Scripture.* This next step—correlation—will give you some answers to interpretive questions as you compare Scripture with Scripture.

7. *Consult a commentary as a last resort.* If you have tried diligently to find the meaning of the text yourself and your cross-references have not helped you, consult the works of great Bible scholars. There is a place for commentaries in Bible study, but it comes *only after you have done your own work.* Compare your interpretation with the writings of devout Christians and see if yours agrees with theirs. If you have a correct interpretation, you may be sure God has shown it to some other sincere Bible students in the past. If you can't find anyone who agrees with you, you have probably got a wrong interpretation.

STEP FOUR *Correlate Your Chapter with Other Scriptures*

This step involves finding cross-references for the verses of your chapter in order to further explain the meaning of the text. It is based on the principle of interpretation that says, "The Bible interprets itself; Scripture best explains Scripture." You can often interpret passages that are not clear by passages that are. Ask yourself, "How do other Scriptures relate to and explain this one?"

Steps in cross-referencing. Here are some practical ways to correlate verses:

1. First, look for cross-references within the same book you are studying. This is *internal* correlation.

2. Second, compare statements in other writings by the same author. This is *external* correlation.

3. Third, compare with other books in the same testament.

4. Finally, compare references in all of Scripture.

You can find cross-references in a study Bible or reference Bible or by looking up similar words in a concordance.

Types of cross-references. There are several different types of cross-references, including the following:

- *The pure cross-reference.* This is sometimes called the parallel cross-reference because it says almost exactly the same thing as the verse you are analyzing.
- *The illustrative cross-reference.* This type, which may involve a real event or person in history, illustrates what the verse you are studying is saying.
- *The contrasting cross-reference.* This type says the opposite of what your verse says. It may look like a contradiction, but it is actually approaching the subject from a different viewpoint.

One word of caution: Be sure to check the *context* of the verses you choose as cross-references. Otherwise you may be making them say what the writer did not say.

STEP FIVE   *List Some Possible Applications*

The last part of the verse-by-verse analysis is to write down some *possible* applications. Remember that your goal in Bible study is not just interpretation but application. Because of the many applications a chapter may have, you will only be *listing* them here. Later on, in Step Seven, you will choose *one* of these to write out and to work on for a week. You have already seen that you cannot work on more than one application per week. It is better to record just one and fully apply that truth to your life than to write down several applications and then fail to implement any of them.

STEP SIX   *Write Down Some Concluding Thoughts*

Go back over the results of the first five steps, review them carefully, and write down some concluding thoughts on the chapter. These can include additional observations, some of your interpretations, themes you have discovered, possible topics and people you want to study in the future, words you may want to do a word study on, and any number of other thoughts that come to mind.

STEP SEVEN   *Write Out One Application*

Now go back to the possible applications you listed in Step Five and choose one of these to work on this coming week. By now you should have had plenty of practice at writing out applications that are personal, practical, possible, and measurable. If necessary, refer back to the Devotional Method of Bible Study (chap. 1). Don't forget to put your application in the present, not future, tense. Ask yourself, "What am I going to do about this *now*?"

HOW TO FILL IN THE CHAPTER ANALYSIS FORM

Use the form at the end of this chapter or write out your study on your own sheet of paper with the necessary divisions.

Filling Out the Form

First, fill in the reference for the chapter you will study. You may want to study only half a chapter if it is a long one. After a few readings, fill in your own title for the chapter, either from your book survey study or a new one that you thought of in these readings. Next, you should summarize the chapter, using one of the three methods suggested in Step One.

As you begin the verse-by-verse analysis, write down the verse numbers in the columns provided and follow that with your observations, interpretations, correlations, and possible applications. Use additional pieces of paper or forms as needed.

On the back of the form write down your concluding thoughts and one application.

Sample Filled-out Form

See the example of Ephesians 1 at the end of this chapter.

Assignment

See the assignment in the Book Survey Method of Bible Study (chap. 9) for suggestions regarding which books of the Bible to study using these three methods.

For Further Reading

More good Bible study books have been written on this method than on any other. As your inclination and finances allow, purchase some of these for your own library and reference.

Good Books on Chapter Analysis

Methodical Bible Study by Robert A. Traina (Zondervan) [Very advanced]
The Navigator Bible Studies Handbook (NavPress)
The New Joy of Discovery in Bible Study by Oletta Wald (Augsburg Fortress)
Personal Bible Study by William Lincoln (Bethany Fellowship)

Good Books on Interpretation

Basic Biblical Interpretation by Roy Zuck (Victor)
Basics of Bible Interpretation by Bob Smith (Word Books)
Getting the Message by Daniel Doriani (Presbyterian & Reformed)
Grasping God's Word by Scott Duvall and Daniel Hays (Zondervan)
How to Read the Bible for All Its Worth by Gordon Fee and Douglas Stuart (Zondervan)
How to Understand Your Bible by T. Norton Sterrett (InterVarsity Press)
Protestant Biblical Interpretation by Bernard Ramm (Baker)
Studying, Interpreting, and Applying the Bible by Walter Henrichsen and Gayle Jackson (Zondervan)

CHAPTER ANALYSIS FORM

CHAPTER Ephesians 1

CHAPTER TITLE God's Great Purpose for Our Lives

1. CHAPTER SUMMARY

Introduction (1:1–2)

I. The Revelation of the Purpose of God (1:3–14)
   A. The summary statement—what he has given us (1:3)
   B. The basis of our salvation (the work of God the Father) (1:4–6)
      1. Chosen to be holy and blameless (1:4)
      2. Adopted as his sons (1:5)
      3. Grace freely given us (1:6)
   C. The benefits of our salvation (the work of God the Son) (1:7–12)
      1. He sacrificed himself for us (1:7)
      2. He lavished grace on us (1:8)
      3. He revealed his will to us (1:9–10)
      4. He made us part of his inheritance (1:11–12)
   D. The bestowment of our salvation (the work of God the Holy Spirit) (1:13–14)
      1. He revealed Christ to us (1:13)
      2. He sealed us as God's children (1:13)
      3. He guarantees our inheritance (1:14)

II. The Response of Prayer to God (1:15–23)
   A. The foundation of the prayer (1:15–17a)
      1. For faithful and loving believers (1:15)
      2. To a faithful and loving God (1:16–17a)
   B. The formulation of the prayer (1:17b–20a)
      1. Prayer for wisdom (1:17b)
      2. Prayer for enlightenment (1:18a)
      3. Prayer for experiential knowledge (1:18b–20a)
   C. The finale of the prayer (1:20b–23)
      Acknowledgment of . . .
      1. Christ's resurrection (1:20b)
      2. Christ's dominion over all (1:21)
      3. Christ's headship over all (1:22)
      4. Christ's lordship over the church (1:23)

CHAPTER ANALYSIS FORM

2. OBSERVATION		3. INTERPRETATION	
What does it say?		**What does it mean?**	
Verse		Verse	
3	God has blessed me with EVERY spiritual blessing.	3	God thinks the world of me.
4	God chose me to live a life of holiness.	4	I must obey God and his commandments.
5	God has adopted me into his family.	5	This means that I belong to him forever.
7	Through Christ I have been forgiven.	7	Christ is the only one who can forgive sins.
9	God has revealed his will to us through Jesus Christ.	9	Christ is God's total revelation of himself.
11	I am made an heir of God through Christ.	11	I have all the privileges of being an heir.
13–14	The Holy Spirit in me is a guarantee of my salvation and acceptance.	13–14	This means I am important, that God gave me so great a guarantee.
16	Paul prays for the Ephesians.	16	I need to pray for fellow Christians.
18	Paul prays for others' enlightenment.	18	I need to pray that others may know God's will.

CHAPTER ANALYSIS FORM

	4. CORRELATION	5. APPLICATION
	Where else is it explained?	What will I do about it?
Verse		
3	1 Peter 1:3 2 Peter 1:4	Thank God for what he has done for me.
4	Romans 8:29 Exodus 20:1–17	I must make sure I'm leading a holy life.
5	Galatians 4:5 Philippians 2:13	I need to act as belonging to God's family.
7	Mark 10:45 Romans 3:25	I must thank God for the totality of his forgiveness.
9	Galatians 1:15 Ephesians 3:9 Hebrews 1:1–2	Bible study is an essential if I'm to know God's will.
11	Romans 8:16–17 Acts 20:32	I should thank God for this great gift.
13–14	John 3:33 Ephesians 4:30 2 Corinthians 5:5	I need to live my life in such a way as not to offend the Spirit who lives in me.
16	Philippians 1:3 Romans 1:8–10	I need to pray for John, Sue, and Bob.
18	Acts 26:18	I need to pray this for Charlie and Gail.

CHAPTER ANALYSIS FORM

6. CONCLUSIONS

This chapter shows what God has given his people—he has blessed them with every spiritual blessing there is. It goes on to list many of those blessings in the Trinitarian work of salvation. This is what God the Father, God the Son, and God the Holy Spirit have done for us. Reading a section of Scripture like this should give us a real sense of worth, because this is God's commentary on what he thinks of those who belong to him.

The proper response to this grand revelation should be a prayer of thanksgiving, adoration, and praise, which is exactly what Paul does.

7. PERSONAL APPLICATION

I need to develop more of the spirit of prayer as Paul does here. He is so overwhelmed by what God has done for us that he spontaneously prays. I need to meditate on what God has done for me and so respond back to him with a prayer of adoration and praise as well.

To implement this, I will reread Ephesians 1 five times, substituting "I" and "me" for the pronouns in the chapter, and then spend time praying without asking anything for myself, but directing all my requests toward God and his glory.

CHAPTER ANALYSIS FORM

CHAPTER

CHAPTER TITLE

1. CHAPTER SUMMARY

CHAPTER ANALYSIS FORM

2. OBSERVATION		3. INTERPRETATION	
What does it say?		**What does it mean?**	
Verse		Verse	

CHAPTER ANALYSIS FORM

	4. CORRELATION	5. APPLICATION
	Where else is it explained?	**What will I do about it?**
Verse		

CHAPTER ANALYSIS FORM

6. CONCLUSIONS

7. PERSONAL APPLICATION

11

THE BOOK SYNTHESIS METHOD OF BIBLE STUDY

How to Tie a Whole Book of the Bible Together

In studying a book of the Bible, we began with the book survey, which examined the book as a whole and came up with a tentative outline of the book. Then we examined the book carefully chapter by chapter, analyzing each verse in each chapter. Now we come to the third of the methods in this three-part approach to studying a book of the Bible. This third method will help you summarize and condense what you have learned from the previous two methods (chaps. 9 and 10).

DEFINITION

The Book Synthesis Method of Bible Study involves studying a book as a whole unit of thought by reading it straight through many times and summarizing its contents on the basis of the previous study and analysis of each of its chapters. "The word *synthetic* is derived from the Greek preposition *syn*, which means *together*, and the verbal root *the*, which means *to put*, so that the resultant meaning is 'a putting together.' Synthetic is the opposite of analytic, which means 'a taking apart' " (Merrill C. Tenney, *Galatians: The Charter of Christian Liberty*, Eerdmans, p. 26). In synthesis we ignore the details and look only at the whole picture. In this method we put together what we took apart in the previous one (chap. 10).

WHY THIS METHOD OF BIBLE STUDY

The Book Synthesis Method is the natural conclusion to an in-depth study of a single book of the Bible. Used in combination with the previous two methods, this study enables you to see the book as a whole again after having looked at its parts in detail. You "put the book back together" so you can see all of the details of the book in the proper perspective. You do this by rereading the book, producing a *final* outline, finding a descriptive title for it, summarizing your overall conclusions about the book, and writing an application.

TOOLS YOU WILL NEED

You will need the same tools for this method as for the Book Survey Method found in chapter 9.

STEP ONE — *Reread the Book*

STEP TWO — *Write Out a Detailed, Final Outline*

STEP THREE — *Write Down a Descriptive Book Title*

STEP FOUR — *Make a Summary of Your Insights*

STEP FIVE — *Write Out a Personal Application*

STEP SIX — *Share the Results of Your Study with Others*

SIMPLE STEPS ON DOING A BOOK SYNTHESIS

The Book Synthesis Form has six steps. Be sure to have handy your previously filled-in Book Survey Form and the Chapter Analysis Forms for each chapter of the book so you can refer to them often.

STEP ONE   *Reread the Book*

Reread the book several times. Read it at one sitting, in a recent translation, rapidly, repeatedly, prayerfully, without referring to commentaries, and with pen or pencil in hand (see the instructions for Step One in chapter 9).

STEP TWO   *Write Out a Detailed, Final Outline*

Compare the horizontal chart and tentative outline you created in your book survey with the passage summaries you created in your chapter analysis studies. Based on this comparison and your recent readings, write out a detailed, final outline of the book. Merrill Tenney gives an excellent example in his book on Bible study methods (Tenney, *Galatians*, p. 35).

STEP THREE   *Write Down a Descriptive Book Title*

From your horizontal chart in the book survey and your detailed, final outline in Step Two, write down a descriptive title for the book you have just studied. Think up an original title that describes in a few words what the book is all about. You might also consult your chapter titles and form a synthesis of them.

STEP FOUR   *Make a Summary of Your Insights*

Review and compare the concluding thoughts in each of your chapter analysis studies and summarize what you believe are the major themes and conclusions of the book. Do not refer to commentaries at this point, for these should be your own insights into God's Word. These insights could also include observations gained from your new readings.

STEP FIVE   *Write Out a Personal Application*

Review all the personal applications you made in your book survey and chapter analysis studies and the possible applications you listed for each chapter. If you haven't fulfilled some of the written applications yet, write those down in this step and make specific plans to carry them out immediately. If you have done them, choose another possible application from the chapter studies or one from your synthetic study and write it out here. Refer to chapter 1 of this book for ways to do this.

STEP SIX   *Share the Results of Your Study with Others*

Bible study should not just be food for your soul and increase your understanding of the Word of God. Its results, including your applications, need to be shared with others. You can do this in two ways:

1. Share with your "Timothy" (or Timothette) in a one-on-one situation. When you get together, share what you are learning from the Bible study, what applications you have been working on, and how he or she too can profit from their own study. The more you give out, the more you will learn yourself.

2. Share with your Bible study group. If you are not in one already, you might want to form a small group in which all of you are studying the same book of the Bible and sharing your findings. This way you will strengthen and help one another in areas of the studies that may not be clear to some in the group.

HOW TO FILL IN THE BOOK SYNTHESIS FORM

Use the form at the end of this chapter to aid you in your study. If you run out of room, attach additional blank sheets to the form so you can keep all of your findings together.

Filling Out the Form

Write the name of the book you intend to study in the appropriate blank. Then follow the six steps of the study as you complete the rest of the form.

Sample Filled-out Form

See the sample on the book of Ephesians at the end of this chapter.

Assignment

Refer back to the "Assignment" section in chapter 9 (Book Survey Method) for suggested biblical books you might start with to practice the three methods described in chapters 9, 10, and 11.

For Further Reading

In addition to the books listed in the "For Further Reading" sections of the two preceding chapters, here are two excellent resources:

Galatians: The Charter of Christian Liberty by Merrill C. Tenney (Eerdmans)
How to Read the Bible Book by Book by Gordon Fee and Douglas Stuart (Zondervan)

——————— BOOK SYNTHESIS FORM ———————

BOOK Ephesians	**CHAPTERS** 6

1. NUMBER OF TIMES READ 5

2. DETAILED, FINAL OUTLINE

Introduction (1:1–2)
- 1. The author (1:1)
- 2. The recipients (1:1)
- 3. The salutation (1:2)

I. God's Plan for the Church (1:3–3:21)
   (Who we are in the sight of God)
- A. The Selection of the Church (1:3–23)
  - 1. The revelation of the purpose of God (1:3–14)
    - a. The summary statement (1:3)
    - b. The basis of our salvation—the work of God the Father (1:4–6)
    - c. The benefits of our salvation—the work of God the Son (1:7–12)
    - d. The bestowment of our salvation—the work of God the Holy Spirit (1:13–14)
  - 2. The response of prayer to God (1:15–23)
- B. The Salvation of the Church (2:1–22)
  - 1. The work of Christ in regeneration (2:1–10)
    - a. What we were (2:1–3)
    - b. What he did (2:4–9)
    - c. What he made of us (2:10)
  - 2. The work of Christ in reconciliation (2:11–22)
    - a. What we were (2:11–12)
    - b. What he did (2:13–18)
    - c. What he made of us (2:19–22)
- C. The Secret of the Church (3:1–21)
  - 1. The revelation of the "mystery" (3:1–13)
    - a. All saved people are heirs together (3:1–6)
    - b. This needs to be preached to everyone (3:7–13)
  - 2. The response of prayer to God (3:14–21)
    - a. Praying for others to know this (3:14–19)
    - b. The doxology (3:20–21)

BOOK SYNTHESIS FORM

OUTLINE (Continued)

  II. The Conduct of the Church (4:1–6:20)
     (What our responsibilities are before God)
    A. The Responsibilities of the Church (4:1–5:21)
       1. To have a united walk (4:1–16)
       2. To have an understanding walk (4:17–32)
       3. To have an unselfish walk (5:1–4)
       4. To have an unsullied walk (5:5–21)
    B. The Relationships within the Church (5:21–6:9)
       1. Marital relationships (5:21–33)
       2. Family relationships (6:1–4)
       3. Employment relationships (6:5–9)
    C. The Resources of the Church (6:10–20)
       1. The admonition (6:10)
       2. The adversaries (6:11–12)
       3. The armor (6:13–17)
       4. The access (6:18)
       5. The ambassador (6:19–20)
Conclusion (6:21–24)
       1. The messenger (6:21–22)
       2. The greeting (6:23–24)

3. DESCRIPTIVE TITLE

"Christian, You Are Somebody! Now Live It!"

BOOK SYNTHESIS FORM

4. SUMMARY OF INSIGHTS

a.   God is the Author of salvation—he planned it from the very beginning. And because it is his plan, it works!

b.   Jesus Christ is the one who redeems us from our sins and reconciles us to God and to one another. There is no way that people of varying backgrounds, races, religions, cultures, etc., can be reconciled to one another except through Christ.

c.   The Holy Spirit is the one who lives in us and enables us to understand what we are in Christ. He is the Guarantee of our salvation and the Enabler for us to live our lives God's way.

d.   Because of who we are in God's sight, we have the responsibility to live holy lives—we have the responsibility to become like him. What God has done is described in chapters 1–3; what we are to do is described in chapters 4–6. We must take these responsibilities seriously.

e.   The plan of God is for ALL his people to be involved in the work of the ministry. Because all of us have been given spiritual blessings, all of us have the responsibility of ministry to others—sharing the gospel, leading them to the Lord, and then discipling them.

f.   God expects a certain type of behavior from all Christians in our most intimate relationships. This includes marriage, raising a family, and where we work. Thus the responsibilities for all of these relationships are carefully spelled out. Our faith is to be expressed through the basic relationships of life.

g.   It is impossible for us in our own strength to live the way God wants. That's why he gave us the Holy Spirit and his armor. The resources of God are ours as well as the blessings. We must put on the whole armor in order to live victoriously.

h.   This book is tremendously heartening to us whenever we begin feeling sorry for ourselves. Here God tells us what he thinks of us. There can be no higher or greater recommendation than God's in terms of what he thinks of us.

─── BOOK SYNTHESIS FORM ───

5. PERSONAL APPLICATION

This book spells out what my responsibilities as a Christian are in all areas of life. I now know that God expects me to be a good and diligent worker. I am to obey him and submit to him in the name of Christ.

I have not always been the best worker. This passage (Ephesians 6:5–9) has convicted me of my responsibility to be a better employee. I will determine, by the help of the Lord, to be the best employee possible for my boss. Also, when the opportunity arises, I will share with him the gospel of Jesus and why this Good News has changed my life. But he's going to have to see it in me first before he will listen to what I have to say.

So that I will carry out this application, I will ask Charlie, a Christian with whom I work, to help me be the kind of worker God wants me to be. I will ask him to meet with me each week to pray that both of us might have that kind of testimony. This may be an opportunity for me to begin working with Charlie on a one-on-one basis.

6. PEOPLE WITH WHOM TO SHARE THIS STUDY

Charlie Johnson

Bud Fredricks

The people in my Bible study group

—————— BOOK SYNTHESIS FORM ——————

BOOK   CHAPTERS

1. NUMBER OF TIMES READ

2. DETAILED, FINAL OUTLINE

BOOK SYNTHESIS FORM

OUTLINE (Continued)

3. DESCRIPTIVE TITLE

BOOK SYNTHESIS FORM

4. SUMMARY OF INSIGHTS

BOOK SYNTHESIS FORM

5. PERSONAL APPLICATION

6. PEOPLE WITH WHOM TO SHARE THIS STUDY

THE VERSE-BY-VERSE ANALYSIS METHOD OF BIBLE STUDY

12

How to Study a Passage of the Bible Verse by Verse

As an alternative to the Chapter Analysis Method of Bible Study (chap. 10), where you use the principles of observation, interpretation, correlation, and application in a systematic fashion, the verse-by-verse analysis of a passage is useful when you don't have the time for an in-depth study. Rather than doing an extensive job on book survey, chapter analysis, and book synthesis, the verse-by-verse analysis of a passage takes each verse and examines it from five viewpoints, using the special Verse-by-Verse Analysis Form.

The five things you will do with each verse are

- Write a personal paraphrase of it.
- List some questions and whatever answers you find.
- Find some cross-references for it.
- Write down some insights you have discovered.
- Write out a brief personal application.

DEFINITION

The Verse-by-Verse Analysis Method of Bible Study involves select-ing a passage of Scripture and examining it in detail by asking questions, finding cross-references, and paraphrasing each verse. You then record a possible, personal application for each verse you study.

WHY THIS METHOD OF BIBLE STUDY

This method may be used two ways. First, it may be used as an alternative to the Chapter Analysis Method when you want to work systematically through a passage or chapter. It is particularly useful when you have limited time and cannot complete a whole chapter at one sitting. In this method you have the option of selecting the number of verses in a passage you want to analyze at any given time. The form is open-ended, and you may proceed at whatever pace you desire.

Second, it may be used in a more advanced topical study. In this case, the verse-by-verse chart would be used in place of the comparison chart at the end of this chapter.

STEP ONE — *Write Out a Personal Paraphrase*

STEP TWO — *List Some Questions, Answers, and Observations*

STEP THREE — *Find Some Cross-References for Each Verse*

STEP FOUR — *Record Any Insights You Get from Each Verse*

STEP FIVE — *Write Down a Brief Personal Application for Each Verse*

This method can be used without reference tools, or you can engage in a more in-depth approach that requires a minimum of tools, as follows:

- A study Bible
- An exhaustive concordance (for cross-references)
- A Bible dictionary and/or Bible encyclopedia
- A set of word studies

SIMPLE STEPS ON DOING A VERSE-BY-VERSE ANALYSIS

This study is built around the verse-by-verse analysis chart. You follow five simple procedures for each verse that you study. To begin, select the passage you want to analyze verse by verse. Work through the passage in a logical order, writing out your first verse in the first space of column 1, second verse in the second space, and so forth (see the sample form).

STEP ONE *Write a Personal Paraphrase*

Write out the verse in your own words. Do not use one of the modern paraphrases except to get the idea of how to do it. Stay true to the verse you are paraphrasing, and try to condense rather than expand it.

STEP TWO *List Some Questions, Answers, and Observations*

In column 3 of the Chapter Analysis Form at the end of this chapter, list any questions you have relating to words, phrases, persons, topics, and doctrines in that verse. Write down any answers you can find and also record any observations you have. Mark these as follows:

- Q = Question
- A = Answer
- O = Observations

STEP THREE *Find Some Cross-References for Each Verse*

Using the cross-references from your study Bible or from Scripture memory, write down some cross-references (at least one) for the verse you are studying. Identify the word or phrase you are cross-referencing at the end of this chapter. Use a concordance if you do not have a cross-referenced Bible.

STEP FOUR *Record Any Insights You Get from Each Verse*

Having thought through the words, phrases, and concepts in the verse, record any insights that you get from them. These could be further observations, words and names that you have looked up and defined, or any other thoughts that come to you. Let your imagination go and be as creative as you can in this fifth column, called Personal Application, in the form at the end of this chapter.

STEP FIVE *Write Down a Brief Personal Application for Each Verse*

Because of the number of verses in your study, you will not be able to design an application project for each verse. Instead, just try to record some devotional thoughts that come to you from each verse. Later, in a devotional Bible study, you can pick one of the thoughts and plan to work on it. Or, if a particular verse seems to meet an immediate need, go ahead and write out an application that is possible, practical, personal, and measurable.

HOW TO FILL IN THE VERSE-BY-VERSE ANALYSIS FORM

You will need as many forms or your own sheets of paper—on which you have drawn the six columns—as there are verses in the chapter you are studying. When you have decided on the number of verses to study, write each one in a separate space in column 1, using your favorite translation of the Bible. You should probably stick with the same translation all through the study.

Filling Out the Form

After selecting the verses and filling in column 1 with their words, fill in the rest of the columns as described in the five steps above. Refer to the sample form for ideas on how to do it. The only limiting factors in this study are your time and your creativity.

Sample Filled-out Form

See the example of 1 Timothy 1:1–3 at the end of this chapter.

Assignment

Since you have been given a sample from 1 Timothy, your assignment is to continue in that book. When you have completed it and want a change of pace after trying some other methods, you may want to study some of the shorter books of the New Testament, such as 2 Timothy, 1 John, Philippians, or the one-chapter books (Philemon, 2 John, 3 John, and Jude).

—— VERSE-BY-VERSE ANALYSIS FORM ——

BOOK OR TOPIC   1 Timothy

Verses	Personal Paraphrase	Questions and Answers
1:1 Paul, an apostle of Christ Jesus by the command of God our Savior and of Christ Jesus our hope,	Paul, one sent forth as Christ's representative, as instructed by God, the One who saves us, and Christ Jesus our hope,	Q. What does the word "apostle" mean? A. The Greek word *apostolos* comes from the verb *apostello*, "send forth." O. God the Father rather than Christ is called Savior.
1:2 To Timothy my true son in the faith: Grace, mercy and peace from God the Father and Christ Jesus our Lord.	To Timothy, my true child in the Christian faith. May love, mercy, and peace from God the Father and Christ Jesus our Lord be yours.	Q. Does the name Timothy have any special meaning? A. Timothy means "he who honors God."
1:3 As I urged you when I went into Macedonia, stay there in Ephesus so that you may command certain people not to teach false doctrines any longer.	As I urged you upon my departure for Macedonia, remain in Ephesus so that you can instruct certain people not to teach non-Christian doctrines.	Q. What doctrines were being taught by these people? A. Not doctrines of false religions, but a false teaching posing as inspired Christian doctrine. Q. What was Timothy's ministry in Ephesus?

VERSE-BY-VERSE ANALYSIS FORM

BOOK OR TOPIC   1 Timothy

Cross-References	Insights	Possible Personal Applications
Apostle: 2 Corinthians 1:1 God my Savior: Luke 1:47 Titus 1:3 Christ our hope: Colossians 1:27	1. The name Paul came from the Latin name *Paulus*, which means "little." 2. The name Timothy means "he who honors God." 3. Paul did not need to tell Timothy that he was an apostle, so perhaps this letter was intended to be read by others as well.	I must begin to see myself in the role of Christ's ambassador who has been authorized and sent out with a divine message. The authority of my witness will only be as effective as my awareness of my mission.
My child: 2 Timothy 1:2 Christ Jesus: 1 Timothy 1:15	1. "Messiah" in Hebrew means "Christo" in Greek, which means "Christ" in English. Christ means "the anointed one of God." 2. Jesus means "Jehovah Saves!" It comes from the word "Joshua."	May my name become synonymous with a life that is honoring to God, like Timothy's.
False teaching: 1 Timothy 6:3 2 Corinthians 11:4	1. Paul criticized the Christians in Corinth for their weakness in dealing with false doctrine (2 Cor. 11:4). Since Timothy was with Paul in Corinth for a long time, he received good training for what was needed in Ephesus. 2. Timothy went to Ephesus with Paul, then later, after Paul's first Roman imprisonment, Timothy was there again. This is when he was urged to stay.	I will endeavor to be knowledgeable of Christian doctrine so I can differentiate between true and false teaching. Christian Science, Jehovah's Witness, and Mormonism all need my attention in this regard.

RICK WARREN'S BIBLE STUDY METHODS

VERSE-BY-VERSE ANALYSIS FORM

BOOK OR TOPIC		
Verses	Personal Paraphrase	Questions and Answers

VERSE-BY-VERSE ANALYSIS FORM

BOOK OR TOPIC		
Cross-References	Insights	Possible Personal Applications

Appendix A

HOW TO HAVE A MEANINGFUL QUIET TIME

Throughout this book I have made references to the quiet time. I have assumed that any person who is committed to personal Bible study also has a regular quiet time. Unfortunately, however, some people do Bible study just for the intellectual stimulation it brings them.

This appendix is for those who know they should have a quiet time but are not sure how to go about it.

The quiet time has been called many things in the history of the Christian church. It is known as the "morning watch," "personal devotions," "appointment with God," or "personal devotional time." It really doesn't matter what you call it as long as you have it regularly.

The quiet time is simply a daily time of personal fellowship with God through the Word and prayer. It is a time we deliberately set aside in which to meet with him. The objective is that we might grow in our personal relationship with God so that we can know him, love him, and become more like him.

This appendix deals with three practical aspects of the quiet time—*why we should have a quiet time, how to have a meaningful time with God,* and *how to deal with common problems* that arise during our quiet times.

WHY SHOULD WE HAVE A QUIET TIME?

"Why" is certainly a legitimate question. What are some good reasons for it? The Bible gives us three major reasons:

- Because we need fellowship with God
- Because it is our privilege as Christians
- Because we gain tremendous benefits from it

BECAUSE WE NEED FELLOWSHIP WITH GOD

The first reason we should have a quiet time is that we need fellowship with God. Because we are Christians, now rightly related to the eternal God of heaven and earth, we must have regular fellowship with him in which we get to know him and love him more intimately.

Why is daily fellowship with God so important?

1. *We were created to have fellowship with God.* God created people in his own image for the purpose of fellowship. We are the only creatures in all creation that have the capacity to have fellowship with the Creator. Adam had that fellowship perfectly in the garden of Eden before the Fall (see Gen. 2–3).

2. *Jesus Christ died on the cross so that fellowship could be restored.* When Adam sinned, his fellowship with God was broken. And all of us sinners who have followed in Adam's footsteps cannot by nature have fellowship with a pure and holy God. But God considered that relationship important enough to send his Son to this world to die for our sins so that we might again have the privilege of a personal relationship with him. And God has called us Christians to have fellowship with him (see 1 Cor. 1:9; 1 John 1:3–4).

3. *The regular quiet time during Jesus' ministry was a source of his strength.* Personal fellowship with his Father in heaven was the top priority of Jesus' life (see Mark 1:35; Luke 5:16; 22:39–44). He was never too busy for it; in fact, when his ministry was the busiest, that's

when he made certain that he kept in daily touch with the Father (see John 5:30). If Jesus needed this time with God, how much more must we need it.

4. *Every great man or woman of God throughout history has spent much time alone with God.* Anyone who has ever been used mightily by the Lord was a person of the Word and prayer. The regular quiet time was the one thing they had in common. The common denominator among Moses, David, Daniel, Paul, John Calvin, John Wesley, Charles Finney, Dwight L. Moody, Charles Spurgeon, Billy Graham, and all of the other great saints of history is that they all spent much time with God in personal fellowship. Their writings and ministries clearly show this.

Someone has said, "If you want to find out what a man is really like, find out what he is like alone with God." Martin Luther, the father of the Reformation, once said, "I have so much to do today that I must spend at least three hours in prayer." The busier he was, the more time he needed with God. If you are too busy to have a quiet time, then you're too busy!

5. *We cannot be healthy, growing Christians without daily fellowship with the Lord.* The quiet time is not just a nice suggestion; it is a vital necessity for a child of God. It is absolutely essential for Christian growth and maturity.

Have you ever gone without food for a day? If you kept it up, you would get weak and sick. The same is true in your spiritual life, for the Bible is the necessary food for your soul. If you go without reading it very long, you will get spiritually weak and sick. Yet many Christians get by with one "meal" per week (for some, perhaps two meals) in church on Sundays. You would not survive long on one or two physical meals per week, so how can you in your spiritual life?

Job considered the Word of God more necessary than his daily food (Job 23:12). Jesus, quoting the Old Testament, declared that people need to live by every word coming from God (Matt. 4:4; see Deut. 8:3). Peter called the Scriptures nourishing milk (1 Peter 2:2), and the writer to the Hebrews thought of the Word as solid food (Heb. 5:14).

Have you ever gone for some time without a bath? If you have, then you know how "sticky" you feel after a while and how your odors get more pronounced. The Bible says that when we read the Word of God, we are cleansed. A daily quiet time is a spiritual bath. Many Christians who would not think of offending their friends by not bathing regularly do not realize that they can be offensive to the Lord with their spiritual odors! (See Ps. 119:9; Eph. 5:26; John 15:3.)

From the above observations, you can conclude that if you are not having a regular quiet time ...

- You are missing out on the privilege for which you were created.
- You are rejecting what Jesus made possible by dying.
- You will never experience the same power and refreshment Jesus did.
- You will never be used greatly by God.
- You will remain a weak and sickly Christian all your life.

"But I don't have the time!" is an excuse we hear so often. Every person in the world has exactly the same amount of time each week—168 hours. You will spend some of those hours on things you think are important. You don't *have* time for everything; you must *make* time for things that really count. It's not a matter of time, but a matter of priorities. What is really important to you?

The key to making time for the quiet time is your commitment to Christ and the kingdom of God. Jesus stated, "Seek first his kingdom and his righteousness, and all these things will be given to you as well" (Matt. 6:33). Put God first in your life and you will have more time. Don't let anything rob you of that time of fellowship with the

Lord. Preserve it at all costs. If Jesus Christ is first in your life, you ought to give him the first part of every day. Your quiet time should be the absolute number one priority and commitment of your life.

BECAUSE IT IS OUR PRIVILEGE AS CHRISTIANS

We should have a quiet time each day because it is a tremendous privilege to have been granted a personal interview and time of fellowship with the Creator of the universe. The quiet time allows us four great privileges:

- We give devotion to God.
- We get direction from God.
- We gain delight in God.
- We grow more like God.

What happens when we have a quiet time?

1. *We give devotion to God.* The first privilege of the quiet time is to *give,* not to get. A psalmist said, "Ascribe to the LORD the glory due his name; worship the LORD in the splendor of his holiness" (Ps. 29:2). Another psalmist urged, "Come, let us bow down in worship, let us kneel before the LORD our Maker" (Ps. 95:6).

In recent years two wrong emphases have been permeating the American church. The first is the overemphasis on *getting*: What will I get out of church, out of Sunday school, out of doing what God says? It is the result of our culture's great emphasis on entertainment, in which the people being entertained must be satisfied. When carried over into spiritual matters, it becomes self-centered religion and is definitely not biblical. That's why so much is being said today about following Jesus, but little is said about the cost of discipleship. We offer prizes to get Christians to come to church when they ought to be coming because they love the Savior.

The other error is the overemphasis on *working* for God and neglecting the *worship* of God. Satan, the god of this world, has sold us a bill of goods in getting us to substitute work for worship. Most of us are so much on the go, even in doing fine Christian things, that we don't know the real meaning of worship. Jesus said, "*Worship* the Lord your God, and *serve* him only" (Matt. 4:10; see Deut. 6:13). Worship comes before service.

We are to give daily devotion to God because God *deserves* our devotion. When John saw the multitudes of heaven singing praises to God, he heard them say, "You are worthy, our Lord and God, to receive glory and honor and power" (Rev. 4:11; see 5:12). Because God is our Creator and Redeemer, he deserves to be worshiped and praised. We should go to our quiet times each day out of love for God, not out of a sense of duty: "God, I've come to worship you because you deserve to be worshiped and adored!"

We are also to give daily devotion to God because he *desires* devotion from us. Jesus told the woman at the well, "Yet a time is coming and has now come when the true worshipers will worship the Father in the Spirit and in truth, for they are the kind of worshipers the Father seeks" (John 4:23). God *seeks* our worship.

A verse that is often used in evangelism, and properly so by way of analogy, was actually written in context to Christians in a lukewarm church. Here Jesus is saying, "Here I am! I stand at the door and knock. If anyone hears my voice and opens the door, I will come in and eat with that person, and they with me" (Rev. 3:20). The Savior *desires* fellowship with us. He stands outside the door of our lives wanting and longing to have fellowship with us and receive our worship. He is like the ideal human father who wants to spend time with his children.

How long has it been since you took time alone with God just to tell him that you love him?

2. *We get direction from God.* The second privilege of the quiet time is for us to get direction from God for daily living. This was David's attitude in life: "Show me your ways, LORD, teach me your paths. Guide me in your truth and teach me, for you are God my Savior, and my hope is in you all day long" (Ps. 25:4–5; see also Pss. 40:8; 73:24; 143:10; Isa. 42:16). The quiet time is a great opportunity to receive counsel from the Lord.

In this fast-paced age of hurry, we need a time when we can slow down, collect our thoughts, evaluate what is happening around us, and get direction from the one who knows the end from the beginning. Pascal once said, "All the troubles of man arise from his inability to sit still." On a number of occasions Jesus invited his disciples to "come apart" with him for a while (e.g., Mark 6:31 KJV), that they might recuperate physically and spiritually. Vance Havner has said, "If you don't 'come apart' periodically, you will literally come apart!" It is also interesting that often Jesus explained his teachings to the disciples when they were alone with him (see Mark 4:34).

When we get direction from God in our quiet times, he causes us first to *consider our ways*. We take the time to assess our lives. That's what David did: "Search me, God, and know my heart; test me and know my anxious thoughts. See if there is any offensive way in me, and lead me in the way everlasting" (Ps. 139:23–24; see also Prov. 4:26; 14:12). Are you keeping on track for the Lord? Are you growing daily in your spiritual life? Have you allowed some sins to pile up in your life? Take these and similar questions and try to look at your life from God's point of view. This will help you keep God's perspective on things, because over and over you can get so caught up in the necessary details of life that you lose the overall picture.

The quiet time is also a time to *commit our day* to the Lord. Solomon urged, "Trust in the LORD with all your heart and lean not on your own understanding; in all your ways submit to him, and he will make your paths straight" (Prov. 3:5–6; see also Ps. 37:5). Ask God to show you his will for the day; commit your schedule to him, and ask him to guide you in the upcoming activities. You might even ask him to help you budget your time so you can get more done (see Ps. 90:12). Ask him to help you sort out the necessary from the unnecessary (see 1 Cor. 10:23).

It is only as you are in touch with the Lord daily that you will see life's problems and opportunities from the right perspective. Only through your meeting with him will he be able to guide your life more effectively. One of the most important requests you can make while committing your day to the Lord is to ask him to prepare you and direct you to someone to whom you can witness that day. Let God pick out your witnessing opportunities.

3. *We gain delight in God.* The third privilege of the quiet time is to enjoy God and simply to bask in his presence. David told God, "You make known to me the path of life; you will fill me with joy *in your presence*" (Ps. 16:11). The secret of real joy is knowing God personally (see Pss. 34:8; 37:4; 42:1–2; 63:1; 73:25; Phil. 3:10). Many Christians are miserable and lead unhappy lives because they never spend time in God's presence.

Do you really *know* Christ, or do you merely know about him? To know him intimately was the apostle Paul's number one priority in life (see Phil. 3:7–10). How is it with you?

To get to know someone intimately and enjoy him personally, you must . . .

- Spend quality time with him.
- Communicate meaningfully with him.
- Observe him in a variety of situations.

These same criteria apply in getting to know and enjoy God, too. Remember that it is hard to have a love affair in a crowd; you need to get alone with that one person. This is why the Bible speaks of our relationship with God through Christ as a love relationship. In fact, it is called a marriage: Christ is the Bridegroom and we in the church are his bride.

When I first met Kay, my wife, and God knit our hearts together in love, more than anything else I wanted to spend time alone with her. We spent time with each other, we communicated, and we observed one another in a variety of situations. That is the way your relationship ought to be with God.

Are you anxious to get alone and share intimately with Jesus? If not, you should be. Make your goal for the quiet time, not just to learn *about* Jesus, but actually to meet *with* him. Expect to meet him each morning, for he's there waiting to meet with you.

Sometimes we get so busy working *for* God or with our own affairs that we forget just to love him. God once said through his prophet, "Does a young woman forget her jewelry, a bride her wedding ornaments? Yet my people have forgotten me, days without number" (Jer. 2:32). We particularly forget God when we fail to read the love letter he has written to us — the Bible.

I once spent a summer on a preaching mission in Japan before my wife and I were married. While I was there, I received a letter from her every day. How do you think Kay would have felt if I told her when I got back home, "Thanks so much for writing me in Japan. I really appreciated receiving your letters. Unfortunately, I never had time to read any of them"? There would have been a strain in our relationship.

The best way to get to know the Lord is to spend time alone with him, sharing your thoughts with him in prayer and reading over and over again the love letter he has written you.

4. *We grow more like God.* The fourth privilege of the quiet time is the opportunity to grow in our spiritual lives, becoming more and more like Jesus Christ. When God created the human race, he "created mankind

in his own image, in the image of God he created them" (Gen. 1:27). His purpose for man was that he might become like God "in [his] likeness" (Gen. 1:26). But man chose to become like the devil instead (Gen. 3). So in the act of redemption God went back to his original purpose. He wanted his people again to be like him, like Jesus Christ. "For those God foreknew he also predestined to be conformed to the image of his Son, that he might be the firstborn among many brothers and sisters" (Rom. 8:29).

How do we become like Jesus? First, we are made holy like God through the Word. In his high priestly prayer Jesus asked the Father to "sanctify [all believers] by the truth; your word is truth" (John 17:17). Our growth in sanctification comes through time spent in the Scriptures, getting to know God intimately.

Second, daily growth comes as the Word builds us up. "All Scripture is God-breathed and is useful for teaching, rebuking, correcting and training in righteousness, so that the servant of God may be thoroughly equipped for every good work" (2 Tim. 3:16–17). As we are taught in the ways of God, rebuked when we go astray, corrected to go back to the right path, and trained in righteous living, we grow in the nurture and admonition of the Lord.

Third, we grow as our minds are transformed from thinking the world's way to thinking God's thoughts after him. Paul wrote, "Do not conform to the pattern of this world, but be transformed by the renewing of your mind. Then you will be able to test and approve what God's will is—his good, pleasing and perfect will" (Rom. 12:2). Again, this comes only through Scripture, God's revelation of his perfect will for us.

Fourth, through the promises of the Word we become more like God. Peter wrote, "His divine power has given us everything we need for a godly life through our knowledge of him who called us by his own glory and goodness. Through these he has given us his very great and precious promises, so that through them you may participate in the divine nature, having escaped the corruption in the world caused by evil desires" (2 Peter 1:3–4). We can only know God and appropriate his promises through the Word.

Fifth, we grow through the help given us by our Christian leaders, who teach us the Word. Paul said that God gives us gifted leaders "to equip his people for works of service, so that the body of Christ may be built up until we all reach unity in the faith and in the knowledge of the Son of God and become mature, attaining to the whole measure of the fullness of Christ" (Eph. 4:12–13).

Finally, we become like Jesus as we spend time contemplating him. Paul wrote, "We all, who with unveiled faces contemplate the Lord's glory, are being transformed into his image with ever-increasing glory, which comes from the Lord, who is the Spirit" (2 Cor. 3:18). This change is gradual; as we keep on contemplating Jesus Christ in his Word, we grow to be more and more like him. It is not a five-second glimpse of Jesus that changes us, but a constant contemplation of him over a period of time.

The more you are with a person, the more you become like him. Have you ever seen a couple happily married for 50 years? They are so much alike by now! They like the same things, eat the same things, and sometimes even start looking alike. The ultimate goal of the quiet time is for us to grow to be just like Jesus Christ.

BECAUSE WE GAIN TREMENDOUS BENEFITS FROM IT

The final reason we should have daily quiet time is the tremendous results it brings to our lives. God has promised many things to those who take the time to get to know him through the Word. What are the results of having a daily quiet time?

- *Joy* (Pss. 16:11; 119:47, 97, 162; Jer. 15:16) — The most joyful Christians are those who meet with God daily.

- *Strength* (Isa. 40:29–31)—As we meet with the Lord daily, we get our spiritual batteries recharged and gain the perspective of an eagle, seeing things as they really are.
- *Peace* (Ps. 119:165; Isa. 26:3; 48:18; Rom. 8:6)—We gain peace of heart only when we have the assurance that God is in control of all things. This assurance comes only through his Word.
- *Stability* (Pss. 16:8–9; 46:1–3; 55:22; 57:7)—When we have a regular time of Bible reading, prayer, and worship, our lives become stable; the quiet time eliminates the "spiritual roller coaster" type of living.
- *Success* (Josh. 1:8)—The only promise of success in the Bible is connected to the condition of daily meditation on the Word of God.
- *Answered prayer* (John 15:7)—As we "remain" in Christ—that is, spending quality time with him daily—we can claim this promise and be assured that our prayers will be answered.
- *Others will notice the difference in our lives* (Acts 4:13)—People will know that we have been with Jesus; it is going to show in our lives. And being with Jesus is what will give confidence and boldness to us in witnessing about him to those who do not know him.

HOW TO HAVE A MEANINGFUL TIME WITH GOD

If we are convinced that we need a quiet time, how do we go about having one? We may become motivated to do it, but may not know how. We need to consider four essential elements of a good quiet time:

- Start with the proper attitudes.
- Select a specific time.
- Choose a special place.
- Follow a simple plan.

START WITH THE PROPER ATTITUDES

In God's eyes, *why* we do something is far more important than *what* we do. On one occasion God told Samuel, "The Lord does not look at the things people look at. People look at the outward appearance, but the Lord looks at the heart" (1 Sam. 16:7). It is quite possible to do the right thing but with the wrong attitude. This was Amaziah's problem, for "he did what was right in the eyes of the Lord, but not wholeheartedly" (2 Chron. 25:2).

When you come to meet with God in the quiet time, you should have these proper attitudes:

1. *Expectancy.* Come before God with anticipation and eagerness. Expect to have a good time of fellowship with him and receive a blessing from your time together. This is what David expected: "You, God, are my God, earnestly I seek you" (Ps. 63:1; see Ps. 42:1):

2. *Reverence.* Don't rush into God's presence, but prepare your heart by being still before him and letting the quietness clear away the thoughts of the world. The prophet Habakkuk tells us, "The Lord is in his holy temple; let all the earth be silent before him" (Hab. 2:20; see Ps. 89:7). Coming into the presence of God is not like going to a football game or some other form of entertainment.

3. *Alertness.* Get wide awake first. Remember that you are meeting with the Creator, the Maker of heaven and earth, the Redeemer of mankind. Be thoroughly rested and alert. The best preparation for a quiet time in the morning begins the night before. Get to bed early so you will be in good shape to meet God in the morning, for he deserves your full attention.

4. *Willingness to obey.* This attitude is crucial: you don't come to your quiet time to choose what you will or won't do, but with the purpose of doing anything and everything that God wants you to do. Jesus said, "Anyone who chooses to do the will of God will find out whether my teaching comes from God or whether I speak on my own" (John 7:17). So come to meet the Lord having already chosen to do his will no matter what.

SELECT A SPECIFIC TIME

The specific time has to do with *when* you should have your quiet time and *how long* it should be. The general rule is this: The best time is when you are at your best. Give God the best part of your day—when you are the freshest and most alert. Don't try to serve God with your leftover time. Remember also that *your* best time may be different from someone else's.

For most of us, however, early in the morning seems to be the best time. It was Jesus' own practice to rise early to pray and meet with the Father. "Very early in the morning, while it was still dark, Jesus got up, left the house and went off to a solitary place, where he prayed" (Mark 1:35).

In the Bible many godly men and women rose early to meet with God. Some of these were

- Abraham—Genesis 19:27
- Job—Job 1:5
- Jacob—Genesis 28:18
- Moses—Exodus 34:4
- Hannah and Elkanah—1 Samuel 1:19
- David—Psalms 5:3; 57:7–8

(See also Pss. 90:14; 119:147; 143:8; Isa. 26:9; Ezek. 12:8.)

Throughout church history many Christians have been used most by God when they met with him early in the morning. Pioneer missionary Hudson Taylor said, "You don't tune up the instruments after the concert is over. That's stupid. It's logical to tune them up before you start."

The great revival among British college students in the late 19th century began with these historic words: "Remember the Morning Watch!" So we need to tune ourselves up at the start of each day as we remember the Morning Watch.

If Jesus is really in first place in our lives, we ought to give him the first part of our day. We are to seek his kingdom first (see Matt. 6:33). Doctors tell us that the most important meal of the day is breakfast. It often determines our energy levels, alertness, and even moods for the day. Likewise, we need a "spiritual breakfast" to start our day off right.

Finally, in the morning our minds are uncluttered from the day's activities. Our thoughts are fresh, we are rested, tensions have not yet come on us, and it's usually the quietest time. One mother sets her alarm clock for 4:00 a.m., has her quiet time, goes back to bed, and then rises when everyone else in the household gets up. Her explanation is that with kids around the house all day, early morning is the only time when it is quiet and she can be alone with God. It works for her; you need to select a time that will work for you.

You might even consider having two quiet times (morning and night). Dawson Trotman used to have code letters for his nightly quiet time: H.W.L.W. Whenever he was with a group of people at night or home with his wife and the conversation seemed to be ending, he would say, "All right, H.W.L.W.," after which a passage of Scripture would be quoted without comment and all would go to sleep. H.W.L.W. stood for "His Word the Last Word," and he practiced that through the years as a way of ending a day with one's thoughts fixed on the Lord (Betty Lee Skinner, *Daws,* NavPress, p. 103).

Stephen Olford, a well-known pastor in New York for many years, said, "I want to hear the voice of God before I hear anyone else's in the morning, and his is the last voice I want to hear at night."

David and Daniel even met with the Lord three times each day (see Ps. 55:17; Dan. 6:10).

Whatever time you set, be consistent in it. Schedule it on your calendar; make an appointment with God as you would with anyone else. Make a date with Jesus! Then look forward to it and don't stand him up. A stood-up date is not a pleasant experience for us, and Jesus does not like to be stood up either. So make a date with him and keep it at all costs.

The question is often asked, "How much time should I spend with the Lord in the morning?" This is a matter to be decided between you and the Lord. If you have never had a consistent quiet time before, you may want to start with seven minutes (Robert D. Foster, *Seven Minutes with God*, NavPress) and let it grow naturally. You should aim eventually to spend not less than 15 minutes a day with God. Out of the 168 hours we all have in a week, 1 hour 45 minutes seems terribly small when you consider that you were created to have fellowship with God. Here are some additional guidelines:

- *Don't try for a two-hour quiet time at first.* You'll only get discouraged. You must grow in this relationship as you do in any other. So begin with a consistent seven minutes and let it grow; it's better to be consistent with a short time than to meet for an hour every other week.
- *Don't watch the clock.* Clock-watching can ruin your quiet time faster than almost anything else. Decide what you can do in the Word and prayer during the time you have selected; then do it. Sometimes it will take more time than you have set aside, and sometimes less. But don't keep looking at your watch.
- *Emphasize quality, not quantity.* There is nothing super-spiritual about having a two-hour quiet time. It's what you do during your time—whether it's 15 minutes or two hours or

something in between—that's important. Aim for a quality relationship with the Lord.

CHOOSE A SPECIAL PLACE

The location—where you have your quiet time—is also important. The Bible indicates that Abraham had a regular place where he met with God (Gen. 19:27). Jesus had a custom of praying in the garden of Gethsemane on the Mount of Olives. "Jesus went out *as usual* to the Mount of Olives, and his disciples followed him" (Luke 22:39). Your place ought to be a *secluded place.* This is a location where you can be alone, where it's quiet, and where you will not be disturbed or interrupted. In today's noisy Western world, this may take some ingenuity, but it is necessary. It ought to be a place . . .

- where you can pray aloud without disturbing others.
- where you have good lighting for reading (a desk, perhaps).
- where you are comfortable. (*Warning*: Do not have your quiet time in bed. That's *too* comfortable!)

Your place ought to be a *special place.* Wherever you decide to meet with the Lord, make it a special place for you and him. As the days go by, that place will come to mean a lot to you because of the wonderful times you have there with Jesus Christ.

Your place ought to be a *sacred place.* This is where you meet with the living God. Where *you* meet the Lord can be just as holy as the place where Abraham met him. You don't have to be in a church building. People have had quiet times in their car parked in a quiet place, in an empty closet at home, in their backyard, and even in a baseball dugout. Each of these places became sacred to them.

FOLLOW A SIMPLE PLAN

Someone has said, "If you aim at nothing, you are sure to hit it!" To have a meaningful quiet time, you will need a plan or some kind of general outline to follow. The main rule is this: Keep your plan simple. Don't let it detract from your time with Christ. Foster's *Seven Minutes with God* suggests a simple plan for beginners.

The following six-point plan is workable for a quiet time of any duration. You will need the following three items:

- *A Bible*—a contemporary translation (not a paraphrase) with good print, preferably without notes.
- *A notebook*—for writing down what the Lord shows you and for making a prayer list.
- *A hymnbook*—in case you sometimes want to sing in your praise time (see Col. 3:16).

The suggested plan may be remembered through the following words, all beginning with the same letter: *relax, request, read, reflect and remember, record, request.*

1. *Wait on God (relax).* Be still for a minute; don't come running into God's presence and start talking immediately. Follow God's admonition: "Be still, and know that I am God" (Ps. 46:10; see also Isa. 30:15; 40:31). Be quiet for a short while to put yourself into a reverent mood.

2. *Pray briefly (request).* This is not your prayer time, but a short opening prayer to ask God to cleanse your heart and guide you into the time together. Two good passages of Scripture to memorize are

- "Search me, God, and know my heart; test me and know my anxious thoughts. See if there is any offensive way in me, and lead me in the way everlasting" (Ps. 139:23–24; see 1 John 1:9).
- "Open my eyes that I may see wonderful things in your law [the Word]" (Ps. 119:18; see John 16:13).

You must be in tune with the Author of the Book before you can understand the Book.

3. *Read a section of the Scripture (read).* This is where your conversation with God begins. He speaks to you through his Word, and you speak with him in prayer. Read your Bible . . .

- *slowly.* Don't be in a hurry; don't try to read too large an amount; don't race through it.
- *repeatedly.* Read a passage over and over until you start to picture it in your mind. The reason some people don't get more out of their Bible reading is that they do not read the Scriptures repeatedly.
- *without stopping.* Don't stop in the middle of a sentence to go off on a tangent and do a doctrinal study. Just read that section for the pure joy of it, allowing God to speak to you. Remember that your goal here is not to gain information, but to feed on the Word and get to know Christ better.
- *aloud but quietly.* Reading Scripture aloud will improve your concentration if you have that problem. It will also help you understand what you are reading better because you will be both seeing and hearing the words. Read softly enough, however, that you don't disturb anyone.
- *systematically.* Read through one book at a time in orderly fashion. Do not use the "random dip" method—a passage here, a chapter there, what you like here, an interesting portion there. You will understand the Bible better if you read it as it was written—a book or letter at a time.
- *to get a sweep of a book.* On some occasions you may want to survey a whole book. In that case you will read it quickly to get a sweep of the total revelation. Then you need not read it slowly or repeatedly.

4. *Meditate and memorize (reflect and remember).* To have the Scriptures speak to you meaningfully, you should meditate on what

you are reading and memorize verses that particularly speak to you. Meditation is "seriously contemplating a thought over and over in your mind" (see chapter 1 for a brief discussion of this).

5. *Write down what God has shown you (record).* When God speaks to you through his Word, record what you have discovered. Writing it down will enable you both to remember what God revealed to you and to check up on your biblical discoveries. Recording what God has shown you is one way of *applying* what you see in the Scripture that pertains to your life (see the Devotional Method of Bible Study in chapter 1).

6. *Have your time of prayer (request).* After God has spoken to you through his Word, speak to him in prayer. This is your part of the conversation with the Lord. To help you remember the parts of prayer, think of the acrostic *P-R-A-Y:*

P—*Praise the Lord.* Begin your time of prayer by praising God for who he is and what he has done. The former is *adoration,* the latter *thanksgiving.* Adoration is real worship; it is giving God the recognition he alone deserves. So praise God for his greatness, power, majesty, strength, and other attributes. Examples in Scripture of pure praise may be found in Psalm 145 and Revelation 4–5. You can worship God in this way by reading the Psalms (particularly Pss. 146–150), reading great hymns of worship, or considering the names of God (see 1 Chron. 16:25–29; Pss. 50:23; 67:3; Heb. 13:5). David gives us a beautiful example of a prayer of adoration in 1 Chronicles 29:10–13.

We also praise the Lord for what he has done for us, particularly in salvation and daily provision. This develops the prayer of thanksgiving. During any quiet time, think of at least 20 things you can thank God for that day. (Read Psalm 100:4; Philippians 4:5; 1 Thessalonians 5:18.)

R—*Repent of your sins.* This is the prayer of *confession.* After seeing God in his holiness (see Isa. 6:5), we recognize our own sinfulness. Don't just tell God about the sins you have committed, but ask him to help you turn away from them. This is repentance. God already knows your sins; he just wants you to admit them and turn away from them. (Read Psalms 32; 51; Proverbs 28:9, 13; 1 John 1:9.)

A—*Ask for yourself and others.* These are the prayers of *petition* and *intercession.* Begin with your own personal requests (petition). Throughout the Bible God urges us to ask for things for ourselves in prayer. These may be physical needs such as food, clothing, and shelter; spiritual needs; or help in coping with the difficult problems of life. God loves us, wants to bless us, and wants to give us what we need (see Matt. 7:7–9; Mark 11:22–24; John 14:13–14; Heb. 4:16). Not only are we to pray for our needs, but God is also pleased to give answers to our desires that are in his will (see Pss. 37:4; 84:11; 145:19; Phil. 4:6).

It is important to be specific in your praying, and one of the ways to do this effectively is to set up a prayer list. Just take a sheet of paper, rule off four columns, and fill them in. As you begin to fill page after page of answered prayer, your faith will grow greater and deeper.

Next, ask for others (intercession). The Bible calls on Christians to intercede for others—to pray one for another. So pray for your family, relatives, and friends; pray for your pastor, church workers, missionaries, and others involved in kingdom work; pray for your leaders, teachers, and employers or employees; pray for people to whom you are witnessing; pray for those whom you do not like or those who do not like you—and watch what happens! (Note these passages: 1 Samuel 12:23; Job 42:10; Romans 15:30; Ephesians 1:15–16.)

You might want to divide up the days of the week in your notebook and pray for different people on different days. Get a world map and pray "around the world" for missionaries according to their location.

Y — *Yield yourself to God's will.* Your prayer time should end with a time of personal recommitment to the Lord. Reaffirm the lordship of Jesus Christ in your life and pledge your submission and obedience for that day to him. (See Rom. 12:12; 14:8–9.)

SOME CLOSING THOUGHTS

- *Vary your plan.* From time to time change your methods. Don't fall into the trap of performing a method instead of getting to know Christ.
- *Spend a whole quiet time in thanksgiving.* Sometimes when prayer seems hard and heavy, spend your time just thanking God for who he is and what he has done. Psalm 145 is a good example of that: the psalmist asked nothing for himself. Or just sing some songs of praise to God.
- *Spend a whole quiet time in Scripture memory.* At times you may want to spend your whole quiet time memorizing Scripture and letting God speak to you in this special and challenging way.
- *Remember your main purpose: to get to know Christ.* Don't let your quiet time become a legalistic exercise in "doing your duty." Remember that you are there to meet Jesus Christ and get to know him.

HOW TO DEAL WITH COMMON PROBLEMS IN THE QUIET TIME

As soon as you start a quiet time or even commit yourself to having one regularly, you will encounter problems and difficulties. Why?

Because Satan will fight you tooth and nail to keep you from your daily meeting with the Lord. He hates nothing more than a Christian getting down to business with God, because he knows that such believers are dangerous to his kingdom of darkness. We want to deal with four of the most common problems:

- The problem of discipline
- The problem of dry spells
- The problem of concentration
- The problem of discouragement

THE PROBLEM OF DISCIPLINE

Perhaps one of the greatest and most common problems you will face is the discipline of getting out of bed in the morning to have the quiet time. It is the "Battle of the Blankets," which faces you the moment you wake up, and it has to do with the question, "Am I going to get out of bed to have a quiet time?"

The devil will exaggerate to you about how tired you are, and when he and the flesh team up, it really takes work to get out of bed. Here are some tips for overcoming this problem.

1. *Go to bed on time.* In order to get up early, it helps to go to bed early (see Ps. 127:2). It's not good to burn the candle at both ends. Many Christians like to stay up late, often watching TV, and therefore have a hard time getting up in the morning. Dawson Trotman knew this and had a set bedtime. Even if he had company in his home, he would excuse himself and go to bed, because his top priority was meeting with Christ early in the morning.

2. *Get up immediately upon waking.* The battle is usually won or lost in the first few seconds. If you wait to think about it, you've already lost. One famous Christian was asked, "Do you pray about getting up to have your quiet time?"

"No," he answered. "I just get up!"

When you wake up in the morning, it is *not* the time to pray about deciding to get up. If you do pray about it, do so the night before, and pray that you will have the willpower to get up.

3. *Be aware of quiet-time "robbers."* Be alert for things that will keep you from having a quiet time. Of these robbers, 90 percent will be found the night before, and of these, TV is the number one culprit. Another robber is the attitude that the quiet time is "nice but not necessary." You must make it a priority in order to thwart the thieves.

4. *Go to bed with thoughts of Scripture.* Go to sleep with the attitude of "see you in the morning, Lord." Ask God to wake you up with your first thoughts on him. The best way to do that is to go to sleep with a verse of Scripture on your mind. Jim Downing, in his book *Meditation: The Bible Tells You How* (NavPress), has some excellent suggestions on how that can be done to enable you to "meditate day and night" (see Josh. 1:8; Ps. 1:2).

THE PROBLEM OF DRY SPELLS

Another common problem of those who have just started having quiet times is that they don't seem to get much out of them. It has become the "Battle of the Blahs." This difficulty may be overcome by realizing that you can never judge your quiet time by your emotions. Emotions may lie; feelings may come and go. So you shouldn't depend on your feelings. If you only have a quiet time when you "feel" like it, the devil will make sure you *never* feel like it.

Yes, some days will seem rather bland. On other days you will think that heaven has opened up and you're part of the innumerable angelic host, singing praises to God. So don't expect to have a great and glorious "experience" every morning. As Billie Hanks says, "It's hard to get spiritual goose bumps in the morning."

Long periods of dryness in your quiet time, however, could be caused by one of the following problems:

1. *Disobedience.* This is unconfessed sin in your life. God won't show you anything new until you do what he has already shown you. If God showed you something in his Word three months ago and you are still fighting it, he won't show you the next step until you've dealt with the first one.

2. *Your physical condition.* Perhaps you haven't been getting enough rest. If you come to your quiet time tired and half asleep, you won't get much out of it. In fact, there is a direct relationship between the physical and the spiritual. Sometimes the most spiritual thing you can do is go to bed earlier each night.

3. *Trying to do too much in a hurry.* The great English Methodist preacher Samuel Chadwick once said, "Hurry is the death of prayer." The same is true with your quiet time. Rushing through it with your eye on the clock will ruin your time with the Lord. Go for quality and content, not for mileage!

4. *Being in a rut.* When your quiet time becomes a ritual instead of a relationship, it's dead. When it is a legalistic exercise instead of a genuine anticipation of meeting the living God, it's in grave danger. This is when you start meeting a habit, not a Person. So be flexible; change your plans and routine, perhaps even your location. But have variety and keep it interesting — to you and to the Lord.

5. *Not sharing your insights with others.* It is a fact of nature that a pond that only receives water but has no outlet will stagnate. The same is true of Christians who are always receiving and never giving. Indeed, it is a divine paradox that when we give out, we get more in return. Start sharing your quiet-time insights with others and see what happens.

If after examining your life and procedures, you are still not getting anything out of your quiet time, tell God about it. Just be honest and admit it to him. Remember that it takes time to develop a relationship with God just as it does with the people around us. You must see him in all kinds of circumstances and get to know him well. Whatever you do, don't give up. Listen to Paul's advice instead: "Let us not become weary in doing good, for at the proper time we will reap a harvest if we do not give up" (Gal. 6:9).

THE PROBLEM OF CONCENTRATION

Once you have won the two previous battles, the devil will attack you by sending many distractions along the way. You will now have to fight the "Battle of the Brain," for your mind will try to wander in all directions during the quiet time. You will be bothered by noises, lack of sleep, poor lighting, tensions with others, worry, and a million other things that you "just can't forget." Here are some suggestions for conquering this problem:

- Be sure you are thoroughly awake. Take a shower, splash cold water on your face, or do some exercises.
- Read and pray aloud.
- Walk while praying. You will not fall asleep standing up, so move around.
- Keep a notebook handy. When you are reminded of something else, write it down and come back to it after your quiet time. Then you won't have to worry about forgetting it.

THE PROBLEM OF DISCOURAGEMENT

By far your greatest problem will be your struggle to stick with your morning quiet time. Nothing is more difficult to maintain regularly, because the world, the flesh, and the devil will work together to keep you from it. When pressures mount and you find that you have too many things to do, what are you usually tempted to drop first? The most important thing—your quiet time.

Satan's most vicious attacks will come in connection with being diligent in your quiet time. He knows that if he can keep you out of the Word, he has defeated you. If he can keep you from spending quality time with the Lord at the start of a day, then he's won the battle, because he knows that he will have no opposition from you.

Dropping your quiet time is usually the first step in spiritual backsliding. Many lukewarm Christians have said, "It all started when I began neglecting my quiet time." That's why Christ stands at their door and knocks, asking for time together (see Rev. 3:20).

In ministering to others, you can never take another person farther spiritually than you have gone yourself. If you have no input from the Lord each day, you will have nothing to share with others and will not be able to help others grow.

How may this serious problem be overcome? Here are some practical suggestions:

1. *Consider making a covenant with God.* Make a serious pact with God to spend *some* time with him during the day. First, however, consider the seriousness of making such a vow. Review Solomon's warning: "When you make a vow to God, do not delay to fulfil it. He has no pleasure in fools; fulfill your vow. It is better not to make a vow than to make one and not fulfill it" (Eccl. 5:4–5). Covenant to have a quiet time, not because others are doing it and not as a duty, but because you know that Jesus Christ wants to meet with you.

2. *Put it into your weekly schedule.* In advance, block out a set time to meet each day with God in the same way you would plan for a doctor's appointment or a business lunch.

3. *Expect and be prepared for the devil's excuses and attacks.* To be forewarned is to be armed. Realize that the devil will try to derail you from your time with the Lord and will attack you on all fronts. So follow the Boy Scout motto and "Be Prepared!" Southern Baptist preacher Robert G. Lee used to say, "If you wake up in the morning

and don't meet the devil face on, it just means you're headed in the same direction!"

4. *Leave your Bible open the night before at the passage you intend to read in the morning.* When you go to bed, open your Bible to the Scriptures you intend to read in your morning quiet time. Then when you wake up in the morning, the opened Bible will serve as a reminder to you to have your quiet time.

CONCLUSION

What if you miss a day? Don't worry about it if it happens occasionally. Don't go on a guilt trip. "There is now no condemnation for those who are in Christ Jesus" (Rom. 8:1). Don't get legalistic, because missing one day does not make it a flop. Don't give up. If you miss a meal, it does not mean that you should give up eating because you're inconsistent. You simply eat a little more at the next meal and go on from there. The same principle holds true for your quiet time.

Psychologists tell us that it usually takes us three weeks to get familiar with some new task or habit; it takes another three weeks before it *becomes* a habit. The reason why many people are not successful in their quiet times is that they have never made it past that six-week barrier. For your quiet time to become a habit, you must have had one daily for at least six weeks.

William James had a famous formula for developing a habit *(Selected Papers on Philosophy,* E. P. Dutton, pp. 60–62).

1. *Make a strong resolution (vow).* You must always start with a strong, decided initiative. If you begin halfheartedly, you'll never make it. Make a public declaration by telling others about your decision.

2. *Never allow an exception to occur until the new habit is securely rooted in your life.* A habit is like a ball of twine: every time you drop it, many strands unwind. So never allow the "just this once"

to occur. The act of yielding weakens the will and increases the lack of self-control.

3. *Seize every opportunity and inclination to practice your new habit.* Whenever you get the slightest urge to practice your new habit, do it right then. Don't wait, but use every opportunity to reinforce your habit. It does not hurt to overdo a new habit when you are first starting.

To these suggestions I would add one more:

4. *Rely on the power of God.* When it is all said and done, you must realize that you are in a spiritual battle and you can only succeed by the power of the Holy Spirit. So pray that God will strengthen you and depend on him to help you develop this habit for his glory.

If you are convinced that this is what you need to do, would you pray the following?

A PRAYER OF COMMITMENT

"Lord, I commit myself to spending a definite time with you every day, no matter what the cost. I am depending on your strength to help me be consistent."

(signed)

GENERAL QUESTIONS FOR A BIOGRAPHICAL STUDY

Here is a list of 70 questions you can use in Step Five of the Biographical Method of Bible Study (see chap. 5). You shouldn't try to use every question in a single study. Depending on the depth of your study and the time you have, select the questions you would most like to have answered. The questions are divided into seven major categories for easier use. As you think of other questions, add them to this list. (For convenience, the questions use masculine pronouns, so substitute feminine pronouns as needed.)

REPUTATION

1. Who wrote what we know about this person?
2. What did people say about him? What did his friends say about him?
3. What did his enemies say about him?
4. What did his family (wife, children, brothers, sisters, parents) say about him?
5. What did God say about him?
6. Why do you think God allowed this person to be mentioned in the Bible?

TESTS OF CHARACTER

7. What were his aims and motives?
8. What was he like in his home?
9. How did he respond to failure? Did he get discouraged easily?
10. How did he respond to adversity? Did he handle criticism well?
11. How did he respond to success? Did he get proud when praised?
12. How did he respond to the trivial and mundane things in life? Was he faithful in the little things?
13. How quickly did he praise God for the good or bad things that happened to him?
14. How quickly did he obey God when told to do something?
15. How quickly did he submit to God-ordained authority?
16. What was he like when he was alone with God?

BACKGROUND

17. What can you discover about his family and ancestry?
18. What does his name mean? Why was he given that name? Was it ever changed?
19. What was his home-life like? How was he raised? Where was he raised?
20. What were the characteristics of his parents? How did they influence him?
21. Was there anything special about his birth?
22. Where did he live? What was his everyday life like?
23. Was he exposed to other cultures? Did they affect him in any way?
24. What was the condition of his country politically and spiritually during his lifetime?

25. What kind of training did he have? Did he have any schooling?
26. What was his occupation?
27. How long did he live? Where did he die? How did he die?

SIGNIFICANT EVENTS

28. Was there any great crisis in his life? How did he handle it?
29. What are the great accomplishments for which he is remembered?
30. Did he experience a divine "call"? How did he respond to it?
31. What crucial decisions did he have to make? How did they affect him? Others?
32. Did any particular problem keep recurring in his life?
33. Where did he succeed? Where did he fail? Why?
34. How did the environment and circumstances affect him?
35. What part did he play in the history of God's plan?
36. Did he believe in the sovereignty of God? (God's control over all events)

RELATIONSHIPS

37. How did he get along with other people? Was he a loner? Was he a team person?
38. How did he treat other people? Did he use them, or serve them?
39. What was his wife like? How did she influence him?
40. What were his children like? How did they influence him?
41. Who were his close companions? What were they like? How did they influence him?
42. Who were his enemies? What were they like? How did they influence him?

43. What influence did he have on others? On his nation? On other nations?
44. Did he take care of his family? How did his children turn out?
45. Did his friends and family help or hinder him in serving the Lord?
46. Did he train anyone to take his place? Did he leave a disciple (a "Timothy") behind?

PERSONALITY

47. What type of person was he? What made him the way he was?
48. Was his temperament choleric, melancholic, sanguine, or phlegmatic?
49. What were the outstanding strengths in his character? What traits did he have?
50. Did his life show any development of character as time passed? Was there growth and progression?
51. What were his particular faults and weaknesses?
52. What were his particular sins? What steps led to those sins?
53. In what area was his greatest battle: lust of the flesh, lust of the eyes, or pride of life?
54. What were the results of his sins and weaknesses?
55. Did he ever get the victory over his particular sins and weaknesses?
56. What qualities made him a success or failure?
57. Was he in any way a type of Christ?

SPIRITUAL LIFE

58. What personal encounters did he have with God that are recorded in Scripture?

59. What was his purpose in life? Did he try to bring glory to God?
60. What message did he preach and live? Was his life a message for or against Christ/God?
61. Did he live a separated life, distinct from worldly ways?
62. What did he believe? What great lessons did God teach him?
63. Why do you think God dealt with him the way he did?
64. What was his attitude toward the Word of God? Did he know the Scriptures existing at that time?
65. What kind of prayer life did he have? Did he have close fellowship with God?
66. Was he bold in sharing his testimony? Was he a courageous witness in times of persecution?
67. How big was his faith in God? How did he show it? Did God give him any specific promises?
68. Was he a good steward of what God had given him—time, wealth, talents?
69. Was he filled with the Spirit? What were his spiritual gifts? Did he use them?
70. Was he eager to do God's will, willingly and without question?

Appendix C

A LIST OF POSITIVE AND NEGATIVE CHARACTER QUALITIES

Listed here are 85 positive characteristics to look for in a person whom you are studying and 113 negative characteristics or sins. These lists will be useful in completing Step Six of the Biographical Method of Bible Study (see chap. 5).

POSITIVE CHARACTERISTICS TO LOOK FOR IN A PERSON

Honesty	Orderliness	Thankfulness
Integrity	Righteousness	Wisdom
Dependability	Fairness	Discernment
Loyalty	Obedience	Sensitivity
Dedication	Courteousness	Perspective
Faithfulness	Respectfulness	Discreetness
Trustworthiness	Reverence	Carefulness
Sincerity	Deference	Cautiousness
Diligence	Gratefulness	Discipline

Thriftiness
Good Stewardship
Resourcefulness
Observation
Industriousness
Creativity
Enthusiasm
Positiveness
Lovingness
Kindness
Patience
Self-Denial
Self-Givingness
Sacrificing
Compassion
Meekness
Sympathy
Generosity
Forgiveness
Gentleness

Mercifulness
Peacemaking
Submissiveness
Agreeableness
Considerateness
Self-Control
Wholeheartedness
Determination
Stability
Energy
Zealousness
Earnestness
Balance
Moderateness
Chasteness
Pureness
Cleanliness
Modesty
Cheerfulness
Optimism

Confidence
Boldness
Courageousness
Faith
Bravery
Durableness
Humility
Calmness
Quietness
Independence
Tolerance
Contentedness
Flexibility
Consistency
Servanthood
Sense of Humor
Characters
   Expressed in the
   Beatitudes

NEGATIVE CHARACTERISTICS AND SINS TO LOOK FOR IN A BIOGRAPHICAL STUDY

Mendacious
Unfaithful
Unreliable
Libelous
Slanderous
Gossipy

Backbiting
Compromising
Flattering
Lazy
Sluggardly
Shallow

Hypocritical
Crafty/Sly
Deceitful
Dishonest
Unfair
Insulting

Coarse	Irritating	Jealous
Rude/Gross	Indifferent	Envious
Impolite	Apathetic	Sarcastic
Rebellious	Idle	Scornful
Meddlesome	Cowardly	Blasphemous
Tyrannical	Copping Out	Bitter
Disobedient	Impulsive	Violent
Ungrateful	Humorless	Complaining
Murmurous	Fickle	Procrastinating
Shortsighted	Double-Minded	Argumentative
Lukewarm	Wavering	Disrespectful
Halfhearted	Headstrong	Manipulative
Foolish	Proud	Bigoted
Talkative	Conceited	Worldly
Idolatrous	Stubborn	Worrisome
Careless	Boastful	Rejoicing in Evil
Forgetful	Sensual	Lustful for Power
Wasteful	Immodest	Self-Righteous
Cruel	Gluttonous	Undisciplined
Inhuman	Inebriate	Apostate
Selfish	Reprobate	Presumptuous
Malicious	Immoral	Profane
Unkind	Unclean	Legalistic
Insensitive	Adulterous	Doctrinally Off
Negligent	Fornicatory	Friendly to the World
Callous	Covetous	Angry without Cause
Prejudiced	Greedy	Ashamed of Christ
Unforgiving	Stingy	Full of Doubt
Harsh	Fearful	Independent in Spirit
Unsociable	Arrogant	Loving of Praise
Grudging	Dogmatic	Forgetful of God
Annoying	Vain	

Appendix D

A PARTIAL LIST
OF BIBLICAL PEOPLE

The three lists that follow include the primary men of the Bible, the secondary but important men of the Bible, and the prominent women of the Bible.

MAJOR MEN IN THE BIBLE

Abraham	Isaiah	Nehemiah
Daniel	Jacob	Paul
David	Jeremiah	Peter
Elijah	Jesus	Pharaoh
Elisha	John (apostle)	Samson
Ezekiel	Joseph (O.T.)	Samuel
Ezra	Joshua	Saul (O.T.)
Isaac	Moses	Solomon

MINOR BUT IMPORTANT MEN
IN THE BIBLE

Aaron	Absalom	Ahithophel
Abel	Achan	Amos
Abimelech	Adam	Ananias
Abner	Ahab	Andrew

Apollos	James	Nathan
Apostles (any)	Jehoshaphat	Noah
Aquila	Jeroboam	Philemon
Asa	Joab	Philip
Balaam	Job	Pontius Pilate
Barnabas	John the Baptist	Prophets (any)
Barzillai	Jonah	Rehoboam
Caiaphas	Jonathan	Shamgar
Caleb	Judas Iscariot	Silas
Eli	Judges (any)	Stephen
Esau	Kings (any)	Timothy
Gehazi	Laban	Titus
Gideon	Lot	Tychicus
Habakkuk	Luke	Uzziah
Haggai	Mark	Zechariah
Haman	Matthew	Zedekiah
Herod	Melchizedek	Zephaniah
Hezekiah	Mephibosheth	Zerubbabel
Hosea	Mordecai	
Jabez	Naaman	

PROMINENT WOMEN IN THE BIBLE

Abigail	Elizabeth	Leah
Abishag	Esther	Lydia
Anna	Eunice	Martha
Bathsheba	Eve	Mary (Jesus'
Deborah	Hagar	mother)
Delilah	Hannah	Mary Magdalene
Dinah	Jezebel	Mary of Bethany
Dorcas	Jochebed	Michal

Miriam	Rachel	Sarah
Naaman's maid	Rahab	The Shunammite
Naomi	Rebekah	Vashti
Priscilla	Ruth	Zipporah
Queen of Sheba	Sapphira	

Also do not forget the nameless women listed as

- "_____'s wife," such as Lot's wife, Potiphar's wife
- "_____'s daughter," such as Pharaoh's daughter
- Various widows and women encountered by Jesus, such as the woman at the well of Sychar

Appendix E

A SUGGESTED LIST OF KEY WORDS FOR STUDY

The following is an alphabetized list of key biblical words that can be used in your Word Study Method of Bible Study (see chap. 7).

Adoption	Evil	Jesus
Adversary	Faint	Judgment
Apostle	Faith	Kingdom
Atonement	Favor	Know
Baptize	Fear	Law
Believe	Fellowship	Laying on of Hands
Bless	Flesh	Life
Body	Good	Light
Call	Gospel	Lord
Chasten	Grace	Love
Christ	Hear	Lust
Church	Hell	Manifest
Confess	Holy	Marriage
Covenant	Hope	Mediator
Death	Immanuel	Meek
Disciple	Iniquity	Mercy
Everlasting	Jehovah	Mind

Minister	Remnant	Spirit
Miracle	Repent	Temptation
Mystery	Rest	Trial
Name	Resurrection	Truth
Obey	Righteous	Understand
Passover	Sabbath	Vain
Peace	Sacrifice	Vision
Perfect	Saint	Watch
Perish	Sanctify	Wisdom
Preach	Save	Witness
Propitiation	Servant	Word
Reconcile	Sin	World
Redeem	Soul	Worship

Appendix F

WHAT TO LOOK FOR IN A CHAPTER ANALYSIS STUDY

Listed here in brief form are 30 items to look for in your observation part of the Chapter Analysis Method of Bible Study (see chap. 10):

1. Ask the six vital observation questions: What? Why? When? How? Where? Who?
2. Look for key words.
3. Look for repeated words and phrases.
4. Look for questions being asked.
5. Look for answers being given.
6. Look for commands.
7. Look for warnings.
8. Look for comparisons — things that are alike.
9. Look for contrasts — things that are different.
10. Look for illustrations.
11. Look for causes and effects and reasons for doing things.
12. Look for promises and their conditions for fulfillment.
13. Look for progression from the general to the specific.
14. Look for progression from the specific to the general.
15. Look for steps of progression in a narrative or biography.
16. Look for lists of things.

17. Look for results.
18. Look for advice, admonitions, and attitudes.
19. Look for the tone of the passage—emotional atmosphere.
20. Look for connectives, articles, and prepositions.
21. Look for explanations.
22. Look for Old Testament quotes in the New Testament.
23. Look for the literary form.
24. Look for paradoxes.
25. Look for emphasis through the use of space—proportion.
26. Look for planned exaggerations or hyperboles.
27. Look at the grammatical construction of each sentence.
28. Look for the use of the current events of the times.
29. Look for the force of the verbs.
30. Look for anything unusual or unexpected.

The above are just a few of the things you can look for in the observation step of your Bible study. Don't let this long list discourage you. You shouldn't try to do each one of the suggested items. It will take time for you to get into the habit of seeing more and more things in the text. The more you practice observing, the more alert you will become. So remember: Look, search, observe, then write your findings down!

Appendix G

A PLAN FOR STUDYING THE BIBLE SYSTEMATICALLY

Once you have committed yourself to studying the Bible personally, you may begin wondering, "What do I do now?" Since there is so much content in the 66 books of the Bible, where should you begin and what plan should you follow?

Each chapter in this book has a suggested assignment for that particular type of Bible study. In this appendix a long-range plan is suggested for studying the Bible systematically. Please use this plan loosely. Don't feel that you have to follow it rigidly. Feel free to change it, to substitute, to omit, to add, and to switch.

The following plan is organized around 48 weeks per year (with four weeks off for vacation) for four years.

YEAR ONE

Weeks 1–4   *Devotional Method:*
    Psalm 15
    Psalm 34
    Romans 12
    1 John 4

Weeks 5–10   *Chapter Summary Method:*
   1 John 1
   2 Timothy 2
   John 17
   1 Corinthians 13
   Ephesians 1
   Haggai 1

Weeks 11–16   *Character Quality Method:*
   Honesty
   Humility
   Servanthood
   Selfishness
   Faithfulness
   Worry

Weeks 17–22   *Thematic Method:*
   The Prayers of Paul
   Obedience
   Knowing God's Will
   Praising the Lord in the Psalms
   The Wise People in Proverbs
   Faithfulness in the New Testament

Weeks 23–28   *Biographical Method:*
   Daniel
   Stephen
   Barnabas
   Gideon
   Ruth
   Nehemiah

Weeks 29–32   *Topical Method:*
   Money — Material Possessions

Prayer
The Family
The Lordship of Christ (doctrinal study)

Weeks 33–36 *Word Study Method:*
Witness
Disciple
Love
Redemption

Weeks 37–38 *Book Background Method:*
The Book of Colossians
The Book of Haggai

Weeks 39–45 *Book Survey, Chapter Analysis, and Book Synthesis
Methods:*
The Book of 1 Thessalonians
Week 39—Survey
Weeks 40–44—Chapter Analysis
Week 45—Synthesis

Weeks 46–48 *Verse-by-Verse Analysis Method:*
Continue on the Book of 1 Timothy

YEAR TWO

From the second year on, you will primarily study books of the Bible,
with the other methods interlaced for a change of pace. You will note
that every time a Bible book is suggested, two more weeks are added
to the number of chapters in that book—for the survey preceding it
and the synthesis following it. Do these in whatever order you desire,
interchanging and substituting freely according to your needs and
interests!

The Book of 2 Timothy	6 weeks
The Gospel of Mark	18 weeks
The Book of Colossians	6 weeks
Four Topical Studies	4 weeks
Four Biographical Studies	4 weeks
Four Word Studies	4 weeks
Verse-by-Verse Chapter Analysis Study of Psalm 145	3 weeks
Three Studies of Your Choice	3 weeks
Total	48 weeks

YEAR THREE

The Book of Philippians	6 weeks
The Book of Romans	18 weeks
The Book of 1 John	7 weeks
Four Topical Studies	4 weeks
Four Biographical Studies	4 weeks
Four Word Studies	4 weeks
Verse-by-Verse Chapter Analysis Study of Psalm 139	3 weeks
Two Studies of Your Choice	2 weeks
Total	48 weeks

YEAR FOUR

The Book of Ephesians	8 weeks
The Book of Acts	30 weeks
Two Topical Studies	2 weeks
Two Word Studies	2 weeks
Verse-by-Verse Chapter Analysis Study of 3 John	2 weeks
Two Studies of Your Choice	4 weeks
Total	48 weeks

YEAR FIVE AND BEYOND

You are now on your own! Pick the books and types of studies that interest you and will help build you up. It is my prayer that these suggestions will motivate you to begin a lifetime of dynamic, personal Bible study.

For Further Reading

Baughman, Ray. *Creative Bible Study Methods.* Moody Press, 1976

Brooks, Keith L. *Basic Bible Study for New Christians.* Moody Press, 1985

_____. *The Summarized Bible: A Guide to Daily Devotional Bible Study.* Baker, 1965

Coleman, Lucien E., Jr. *Developing Skills for Bible Interpretation.* The Sunday School Board of the Southern Baptist Convention, 1969

Corley, Bruce, Steve Lemke, and Grand Lovejoy, eds. *Biblical Hermeneutics.* 2nd ed. Broadman & Holman, 2002

Downing, Jim. *Meditation: The Bible Tells You How.* NavPress, 1977

Glynn, John. *Commentary and Reference Survey: A Comprehensive Guide to Biblical and Theological Resources.* Kregel, 2003

Henrichsen, Walter A., and Gayle Jackson. *Studying, Interpreting, and Applying the Bible.* Zondervan, 1990

Jensen, Irving L. *Enjoy Your Bible.* World Wide Publications, 1989

_____. *Independent Bible Study.* Moody Press, 1972

Job, John B., ed. *How to Study the Bible.* InterVarsity Press, 1973

Klein, William, Craig Blomberg, and Robert Hubbard. *Introduction to Biblical Interpretation.* Rev. ed. Nelson, 2004

LaHaye, Tim. *How to Study the Bible for Yourself.* Harvest House, 1988

Lincoln, William C. *Personal Bible Study.* Bethany Fellowship, 1975

McCartney, Dan, and Charles Clayton. *Let the Reader Understand.* 2nd ed. Presbyterian & Reformed, 2002

Mickelsen, A. Berkeley. *Better Bible Study.* Regal Books, 1977

Miller, Park Hays. *How to Study and Use the Bible.* W. A. Wilde, 1954

Navigator Bible Studies Handbook, The. NavPress, 1995

Perry, Lloyd and Robert D. Culver. *How to Search the Scriptures.* Baker, 1967

Ramm, Bernard. *Protestant Biblical Interpretation.* Baker, 1980

Ramm, Bernard, ed. *Hermeneutics.* Baker, 1987

Robertson, Edward H. *Methods of Bible Study.* The Bible in Our Time Series. Association Press, 1962

Smith, Bob. *Basics of Bible Interpretation.* Word Books, 1978

Smith, Wilbur M. *Profitable Bible Study.* Baker, 1971

Sproul, R. C. *Knowing Scripture.* InterVarsity Press, 1977

Sterrett, T. Norton. *How to Understand Your Bible.* InterVarsity Press, 1982

Torrey, R. A. *How to Study the Bible for Greatest Profit.* Baker, 1984

Traina, Robert A. *Methodical Bible Study.* Zondervan, 1985

Wald, Oletta. *The New Joy of Discovery in Bible Study.* Augsburg Fortress, 2002

Wollen, Albert J. *Miracles Happen in Group Bible Study.* Regal Books, 1976

Share Your Thoughts

With the Author: Your comments will be forwarded to
the author when you send them to *zauthor@zondervan.com*.

With Zondervan: Submit your review of this book
by writing to *zreview@zondervan.com*.

Free Online Resources at
www.zondervan.com

Zondervan AuthorTracker: Be notified whenever your favorite
authors publish new books, go on tour, or post an update
about what's happening in their lives at www.zondervan.com/
authortracker.

Daily Bible Verses and Devotions: Enrich your life with daily
Bible verses or devotions that help you start every morning
focused on God. Visit www.zondervan.com/newsletters.

Free Email Publications: Sign up for newsletters on Christian
living, academic resources, church ministry, fiction, children's
resources, and more. Visit www.zondervan.com/newsletters.

Zondervan Bible Search: Find and compare Bible passages in
a variety of translations at www.zondervanbiblesearch.com.

Other Benefits: Register to receive online benefits like
coupons and special offers, or to participate in research.